BIBLE HEROES

NOAH/JOSEPH
DAVID/DANIEL

BARBOUR
PUBLISHING, INC.
Uhrichsville, Ohio

© 2001 by Barbour Publishing, Inc.

ISBN 1-58660-130-X

Noah by Susan Martins Miller. © 1999 by Barbour Publishing, Inc.
Joseph by Rex Williams. © 1990 by Barbour Publishing, Inc.
David by Sam Wellman. © 1999 by Sam Wellman.
Daniel by Ellen Caughey. © 1998 by Barbour Publishing, Inc.

Published by Barbour Publishing, Inc., P.O. Box 719, Uhrichsville, Ohio 44683
http://www.barbourbooks.com

ecpa Member of the
Evangelical Christian
Publishers Association

Printed in the United States of America.

CONTENTS

NOAH

BUILDER OF THE ARK

by Susan Martins Miller

CHAPTER 1

The camel hair blanket scratched the old man's bearded cheek. After working in the fields all day, he should be tired. And his body was tired. His arms and legs ached from his labor. His neck was so stiff he could barely lift his head off the pillow. His eyes had been shut for a while, but behind his closed eyes, the old man's mind was wide awake. His brain churned out one thought after another.

Sighing, he pushed the scratchy blanket away from his face. Noah had a funny feeling. Something nagged at his brain. He was overlooking something important, but he could not figure out what it was. He knew he would never be able to sleep until he figured out what was keeping him awake.

In his mind, he went over the day. He had fed the livestock in the morning. The grain bin was almost empty, so he had looked for his son Shem to ask him to fill it. But he had not seen Shem all day. Noah would have to remember tomorrow to remind Shem, or the animals would have nothing to eat.

After tending the animals, Noah had gone out into the fields to inspect the crops. Ham and Japheth, his other two sons, met him there. They agreed that they would have a fine harvest this year. Nothing was wrong with the crops, and Shem would eventually remember to feed the animals. What was keeping Noah awake?

Sighing, Noah heaved himself over to one side. He was six hundred years old. He was an old man, a tired old man who still worked hard every day. He ought to be sleeping. Why wasn't he? He kicked at the blanket.

When he came in from the fields for the midday meal, his wife was flustered. She would not say why. Noah had stroked her back and tried to soothe her. He suspected she was worried about the missing Shem.

"Is his wife gone, too?" Noah asked.

His own wife grunted.

"It is nothing," Noah said softly. "They have gone off to spend the day together."

"There is work to be done," his wife answered. She poured thick soup into a dish. "I saw you feeding the animals this morning."

"And Shem will do his work," Noah said confidently.

"It is time for the boy to show some responsibility."

"He is not a boy. He is a man. All our boys are men," Noah reminded his wife. "They have their own wives. They have brought us the daughters we did not have. God has blessed us."

Noah's wife turned and looked him in the eyes. "I am always amazed at how deeply you believe in God," she said. "When I look around, I see evil, pure evil. People are killing each other, cheating each other, lying, stealing, disobeying every law anyone ever made. Yet you believe God has blessed us."

Noah picked up a bowl of soup and set it on the table. "God has blessed us. All the things you say are true. Many days, I am as frightened as you are to leave the safety of our home." His eyes widened. "That is why you are concerned about Shem."

She turned away again and filled another bowl with soup. "What if he does not come back?"

"He will come back. He always does."

"What if today he does not?"

"God will keep him safe."

"Noah, you are closer to God than anyone I know. In fact, outside of our family, I do not know anyone who believes in God."

"God walks with me wherever I go." Noah broke off a piece of bread and said no more.

They ate their lunch in silence, listening for any sound of Shem's safe return. He had not come home all day. Ham and Japheth and their wives did not know where the missing couple had gone.

Lying in the dark that night, Noah breathed in the sweet scent of his wife sleeping peacefully next to him. She had worried herself into exhaustion. It was the middle of the night, and she was sound asleep—just like she was supposed to be. Noah shook his head and turned over once more.

Then he heard it. His eyes, wide open, darted around the dark room. There it was again. He could not see it, but he knew something was there. Holding his breath, he listened.

No one else would hear it. But Noah heard it.

He did not know how long it lasted. It might have been only a few seconds or several hours. Noah sat bolt upright, nearly knocking the blanket off the mattress he shared with his wife.

"Noah!" his wife said sharply.

Noah cringed. His wife did not like to be awakened in the middle of the night without a very good reason.

"What in the world is going on?" she demanded. "You are thrashing about like you are harvesting wheat. And all that sighing and moaning and singing—you're making too much noise."

"Singing? I was singing?" Noah asked.

"You always insist you have a song in your soul. But I don't understand why your soul cannot be quiet at night."

Noah smiled. If he was singing, then it was true. What he had heard was a holy moment.

"You are not going to believe what just happened," Noah told his sleepy wife.

"If I am not going to believe it anyway, you might as well wait for morning to tell me," she answered groggily.

"Yes, yes, in the morning," Noah agreed. "The boys, too. We must get the boys together."

"I thought you said they were men," his wife answered.

"Yes, and their wives. You must all know."

"Why don't we invite the neighbors, too? Perhaps they are interested in your middle-of-the-night adventures."

Noah paid no attention to his wife's harsh tone. "No, no, not the neighbors. No one from town. Just the family."

"Good. Just the family." His wife was drifting back to sleep. "Whatever you say. Just be still and let me sleep."

Noah patted his wife's shoulder. "Yes, I will try to be still."

He lay back down in the bed and crossed his arms across his chest. Now he was more awake than ever. What did it all mean? What God had said to him in the night was a message for a young man. *I am so old,* Noah told himself. *Perhaps I am losing my mind. Even if I were three hundred years younger, I would find this hard to believe.*

But Noah had walked and talked with God every day for six hundred years. He knew when God spoke. And he knew that he would obey. No matter how ridiculous the message sounded, Noah would do what God asked him to do. He would need the help of his sons. The job was far too big for one old man. But he would obey.

Silently, he repeated to himself what he had heard. He said the words over and over. He no longer wanted to sleep. He wanted to remember every word.

Noah plunged his hands into the water trough and splashed cool refreshment on his face. His sleepless night was catching up with him. But at least Shem had come home. When Noah went out to feed the animals in the morning, Shem was there. The feeding bins were full of grain. Shem stood among the chickens, throwing out handfuls of feed, singing as he worked.

Noah worked alongside Shem all morning. They tended the animals together and walked through the fields checking on the crops. Shem did not say where he had been, and Noah did not ask. He was just glad Shem had come home. Now he would be able to talk to all three of his sons and their wives at the same time.

The morning passed quickly. Now Noah was cleaning up for lunch. He could hear his wife scolding Shem for making her worry. Shem only laughed and kissed his mother sloppily on one cheek. Noah smiled at the familiar sight.

He had good sons, sons to be proud of. Nearly every time he went into town, Noah heard a new story about someone's son who had stolen or murdered someone else's son. He saw the bribes passed under the tables in the marketplace. He heard the lies that the merchants told so that they could sell more of their goods. He ached with other fathers whose sons ran off and never came home again. Yes, Noah had good sons. The Lord had blessed him.

Japheth stuck his head out the door and called, "Father, the meal is ready."

"I'll be right there," Noah responded. He splashed his face one more time and then dried his hands and face on a clean cloth. As he turned to enter his home, he took a deep breath. Would his family believe what he had to say?

Inside, he took his seat. Around the table, his whole family was gathered. Shem, Ham, and Japheth sat with their wives. His own wife sat at the far end of the table. Before them was a meal of roasted lamb and bread.

Noah smiled at his family. "God has provided for us another day," he said. And they began to eat.

His wife raised the platter of meat and handed it to Ham. "Noah, are you going to explain what all that fuss was about in the middle of the night?"

Noah was caught off guard. He had expected to bring up the subject himself. His wife's question forced him to try to organize his thoughts.

Japheth put two thick slices of bread on his plate. "What fuss?" he asked. "I didn't hear anything."

"That's because you were not sleeping next to your father," his mother answered.

Japheth turned toward Noah. "Is something wrong, Father?"

Everyone's eyes were fixed on Noah.

"No, no, nothing is wrong," Noah began. "But I do have something to tell you all. It's difficult to explain."

Shem passed the platter of lamb to his wife. "You might as well try, while we're all here."

Noah pushed his empty plate away. Suddenly he was not very hungry. He looked around the table, knowing that he should say something soon.

"What is it, Father?" Ham asked.

"God spoke to me last night," Noah said quietly.

"God? Are you sure?" Japheth asked.

"Yes, I'm sure. God has spoken to me before. I know the voice of the Almighty."

"What did he say?" Shem's wife asked.

Noah closed his eyes. "He said He is going to destroy the earth," he said quietly. "Every living creature will perish."

Around the table, no one spoke. Noah opened his eyes. His whole family was staring at him. He knew what they were thinking.

"I assure you, I have not lost my mind," Noah said firmly.

"Destroy the earth?" Ham said. "The entire earth?"

"That is what He said. Because the earth is filled with violence, God is going to destroy it. He gave me instructions to build an ark."

"An ark?" Japheth echoed.

"Yes, an ark. A big boat. A huge ship."

"Then not everything is to be destroyed," Shem said.

"We are to be spared," Noah said. "Only us. God is making

a covenant with me. My wife, my sons, and my sons' wives will be spared. We will take with us into the ark two of every kind of animal, and seven of every kind of bird. After the flood, the animals will breed and fill the earth again."

"Flood?" his wife asked.

"Yes, a flood," Noah answered. "God is going to bring flood waters on the earth to destroy every living creature, except what is in the ark."

"Just how big is this ark?" Ham asked.

"Very big," Noah answered. "It will be 450 feet long, seventy-five feet wide, and forty-five feet high. It will have a roof, of course, and we will build the sides of the ark up to within eighteen inches of the roof."

"That's big," Japheth agreed. "But the animals—we can't just throw them in that empty space."

"We'll build decks," Noah went on. "We'll have a lower deck, a middle deck, and an upper deck. Each deck will be divided into rooms. We'll have living quarters, of course. And the animals will be arranged in a way that keeps the smaller ones safe."

"With that many animals in one place, I hope we'll have windows for fresh air," Shem said.

"We'll have a row of windows just under the roof," Noah said, "and one door."

Noah looked around the table. His sons avoided his eyes. They looked at each other with questions in their eyes.

"I know what you are thinking," Noah said. "I am an old

man, and I have had an old man's dream. You think that maybe the spicy stew last night upset my stomach and gave me nightmares. But this is no dream. Haven't I always told you the truth? I am telling the truth now."

"Of course you are, Father," Japheth said, after a long silence. "We know you would not tell us something you knew was a lie. It's just—"

"It's just incredible," Shem blurted out. "We need some time to understand what you are saying."

"I can repeat it, if you want me to," Noah said. "But we do not have much time. We must begin working right away."

"How long will we be in this ark?" Shem's wife asked.

Noah shook his head. "I don't know the answers to all your questions. We will take every kind of food that we can. We will need to begin storing food right away."

"What if it is not enough?" Shem asked. "We'll have all the animals to feed, too, after all."

"It will be enough. God always provides enough." Noah looked around the table. No one had eaten much of the carefully prepared meal. "I know this is incredible," he said. "You want to believe me, but it is hard. Don't believe me. Believe God. What He has said will happen."

Noah dragged his arm across his forehead and wiped the sweat on his sleeve. He had never worked so hard in all of his six hundred years.

It had taken him days to calculate how much wood it would take to build the ark. Shem and Ham asked him where he planned to get that much wood. He told them it would be their responsibility to get it. He grinned as he said it. Their jaws dropped open in protest, and that made Noah laugh. But they began to gather the wood. First they bought as much as they could. They went to everyone they knew who might have a pile of wood and asked if he had any gopher wood for sale. If the wood was already cut, they could save a lot of work, although they still had to move it to their own property.

Next, they had to look for forests where they could cut the rest of the wood they needed. They hiked for days looking for just the right wood. Their father's instructions were very specific. It had to be gopher wood. They hired a team of strong young men with saws and axes. Ham and Shem marked the trees they wanted, and the men went to work. They chopped the trees, sawed them into flat boards, and hauled the wood to Noah's property.

Japheth helped his father at the work yard. Noah repeated the instructions for the ark so many times that Japheth knew them as well as his father. They had the same picture in their minds of what the ark would look like when it was finished. As the project grew, Japheth was amazed at how long 450 feet was. He himself felt smaller by the day. They had fenced off a huge work yard. Now Japheth was sure the space would be too small.

Almost as soon as they began to build, Japheth convinced Noah that the job was too big for just the two of them. They hired day workers who came and followed their directions. At first, Japheth did not want to tell anyone what they were building. Who would believe them? On some days, he could hardly believe it himself. He trusted his father, but other people would not be so understanding.

Japheth just told the workers where to put the boards and how to fasten them together. He waited for the day when they would insist he answer their questions. The workers had many ideas about what the project might be. Japheth paid no attention to their guesses.

The day came when Noah and Japheth had to mix a huge vat of pitch. The tarry, smelly, sticky goo would make the ark waterproof. The workers put their tools down and lined up in front of Noah and Japheth.

"You must tell us what we are building," one of the men said. "You can't expect us to work with that awful stuff if you don't tell us what we are doing."

Japheth glanced at his father. "We're paying you to do what we tell you to do. You don't have to stay if you don't want to."

None of the men moved. The leader glared at Japheth.

"Hazar," Japheth said, "take your men and go back to work."

"Not until you tell us what we're building."

Japheth shook his head. He did not want to tell them. But Noah stepped forward.

"We're building an ark," he said, "and the pitch is to make it waterproof."

"An ark?" Hazar asked skeptically.

"An ark—a big, flat boat."

Some of the men began to snicker. "A boat this big?" one said. "We're nowhere near the ocean, and you've never been a sailor. What do you need with a huge boat?"

"If you are really interested, I'll be happy to explain it to you," Noah said calmly. "But the news is not good."

"What news?"

"Father, please," Japheth said, laying his hand on his father's arm. "Please don't say anything more."

Noah turned to his son. He spoke quietly. "Don't you think we owe them an explanation?"

"We owe them nothing, except their wages," Japheth insisted.

"I know what you are thinking," Noah said. "Who will believe us? They will think we are a family of crazy people."

"What is the point of trying to explain?" Japheth said.

Noah shrugged. "We cannot do all this work ourselves. If we want them to stay, we must answer their questions."

"If we answer their questions, they will run in fear," Japheth said.

"Only if they believe us. I don't think they will." Noah spoke sadly.

"But they will laugh at us," Japheth said. "Listen. They have already begun to laugh at the mention of the ark."

"Let them laugh." Noah straightened his shoulders. He sighed and turned back to the workers. "We are building an ark because there is going to be a flood that will cover the whole earth. Everything that we know will be destroyed. Nothing will be left except what is in the ark. God has told me that—"

Noah could not finish what he started to say. The whole group had burst into laughter.

Hazar smirked at Japheth. "I can see why you did not want the old man to speak. A flood that destroys the whole earth?"

Behind Hazar, another voice roared. "Your father is a crazy old man, Japheth. But I thought better of you—until now."

"My father is—" Japheth started to speak, but his father touched his arm and shook his head.

"No, Japheth. You are right. They will not listen to the truth," Noah said sadly.

Hazar threw a log on the fire under the vat of pitch. The oozing mixture gurgled and popped. "If you are crazy enough to keep paying us to work on this monstrosity, then I guess we'll do it. But don't complain later that we tried to cheat you." The other men joined Hazar in a fresh round of laughter.

Japheth sighed. The men would no longer just follow his instructions. He would have to put up with their ridicule every day until the ark was done.

"Let's all just get back to work," Japheth said. He picked up a long stick to stir the pitch.

Snickering, the men returned to their tasks.

Japheth turned to his father. "We have a long time before this job will be finished. Shem and Ham haven't even found all the wood we need yet. How are we going to put up with everyone laughing at us? I'm sure they will be stealing from us every chance they get, too, and lying about everything they do."

Noah nodded. "I know, Japheth. I may be old, but I am not as foolish as they think I am. But I don't care if they laugh. I am obeying what God told me to do. That's all that matters."

"But what about the stealing and lying?" Japheth asked.

"Why does it matter? Have you forgotten what will happen when the flood comes?" Noah asked.

Japheth nodded. "The world will be destroyed."

CHAPTER 4

Noah straightened his shoulders and tried to tell himself he was not tired. It was the heat that wearied him, he told himself. If he could just stand in the shade for a few minutes, he would feel better.

He raised one arm and wiped the sweat from his face with his garment. Squinting into the afternoon sun, he chose the tree he would stand under. Slowly, he shuffled toward the spreading cedar tree. Just thinking about its cool shade made him feel better. When he reached the tree, he sank down on the ground and leaned against the thick trunk. He would close his eyes just for a few moments. Surely that would refresh him.

Behind him, the workers continued their labor in the sun. The walls of the ark had risen, foot by foot, until they stood forty-five feet high. The last part of the walls was almost finished. Soon it would be time for the roof. Noah was pleased with the progress. He was sure he had followed every instruction God had given. Noah leaned his head back against the tree and closed his eyes.

Watching him, two of the workers laid down their tools.

"Look at him," one of them said. "It's only midmorning, and he's worn out already."

"He's an old man," the other replied. "He has no business getting involved in a project like this."

"He's more than old," the first one answered. "He's old and crazy. All this talk about a flood is ridiculous."

"I wonder if we're not crazy, too. We keep coming back to work on his crazy boat."

"He doesn't like it when you call it a boat. It's an ark."

"Okay, but it's a crazy ark. Why do we keep working on it?"

"Because he keeps paying us. And he pays very well."

"He must be using up everything he ever saved in his whole life." The man laughed. "I wonder why his sons don't protest. It's their inheritance the old man is wasting."

The other man shrugged. "They don't seem to mind. They say none of them are going to need gold or silver after the flood."

"Won't they be surprised when they have nothing left, and there is no flood. How could anything destroy the whole earth? Such a bunch of fools!"

Their voices faded as the two men picked up their tools and wandered back to their work.

Noah opened his eyes. He had heard everything they said. He did not blame them. If he were a strong young man who had not yet walked with God, he might think the same thing. Noah knew lots of other very old men who got some crazy ideas into their heads. They could not tell the difference between what was real and imaginary. Why should anyone think he would be any different? But he wasn't crazy. And the least he could do was work as hard as anyone else.

With a sigh, Noah pulled himself to his feet. He turned back to the work yard and tried to think what needed to be done. There was a stack of wood that should be moved closer to the fire under the bubbling, stinky pitch vat. He would work on that. No one else seemed to like to go near the pitch vat. Noah leaned down and began filling his arms with wood.

When he could barely see over the armload of wood, he added one more piece to the pile. Stumbling, he began to make his way toward the fire. Noah could feel the eyes of the younger men fixed on him as he passed them, slowly but steadily. He could see the fire, but it seemed like it was miles away instead of only a few yards. Maybe those younger men were right; maybe he was a silly old man. Why had he tried to carry so much at one time? Breathing heavily, he continued.

"Father, let me help you." Shem was beside his father and began snatching wood from Noah's arms. Noah did not protest. He let Shem take nearly the whole load, till he carried only four small pieces in his own arms. Together, they moved toward the fire and dumped the logs on the ground.

"Father, let's sit down and rest," Shem suggested.

Noah shook his head. "No, I just had a rest."

"But I need one," Shem insisted, "and I want to talk to you."

Noah reluctantly agreed. Side by side, they sat on a low bench.

Shem sighed.

"What is wrong, my son?" Noah asked.

"It's these men," Shem answered. "They think this is just another job. They believe that when the ark is finished, they will move on and find other work."

Noah shook his head. "It is sad."

"But you have said that everything will perish," Shem went on. "You said that God will destroy all life under the heavens, and every creature that has the breath of life in it."

"I only told you what God told me," Noah said. "It was not my decision to destroy the earth."

"But God chose to spare you," Shem continued, "and because He is sparing you, He is sparing me also. I can't help but think about what is going to happen to everyone else I know."

Noah let his shoulders sag and exhaled. "It is sad. But all these people have had their chance to know God. They have not chosen to walk with Him, as I have, and as you have."

"I know that is true, Father," Shem said. "I have no real friends, because I don't know anyone I can trust."

"Everyone is corrupt."

"You can't get anything done without a bribe. All the merchants try to cheat you. Every time a group of people gathers, a fight breaks out. Most of the time, somebody ends up dead."

"All of this displeases God. That is why He is going to destroy the earth."

"Shouldn't we be trying to convince people to change their ways?" Shem asked. "There is room in the ark for more, isn't there? Or we could make it bigger."

Noah shook his head sadly. "No. God has spoken. He has given the size of the ark, and He has said that only our family will enter the ark." He lifted his eyes. "Here comes your wife now."

Shem looked to see his wife lugging an animal skin, stretched and tanned. Besides the crew building the ark, another group of people worked at tanning animal hides.

"My wife tells me that we have almost enough hides for the roof now," Shem said.

"Good," Noah responded. "We'll be ready for that soon. And the food supply?"

"The women are gathering grain. They have sacks and sacks of it, and baskets of fruits and vegetables. They have meat hanging to dry. We should have plenty to eat."

Noah nodded in satisfaction and raised his eyes to the sky. "It won't be long."

CHAPTER 5

The work yard was quiet. Still convinced that Noah had lost his mind, the men had taken their tools and gone on to another job. Their work for Noah was finished.

"We did exactly as he asked," said Hazar, the work crew leader, "and I've never seen an uglier boat in all my life."

"It's not a boat," someone corrected Hazar. "It's an ark."

"It's a monstrosity. No one can argue with that."

The men roared with laughter. Noah said nothing. He had grown used to the ridicule. What the work crew or the neighbors thought did not matter. What did matter was that the ark was done. The work crew had followed every detail, even though they thought it was ridiculous. They had done everything right.

Noah and his sons stood alone in the work yard. The enormous ark loomed over them.

Japheth kicked an empty bucket. "I suppose we should clean this mess up," he said. "They left wood shavings and scraps from the animal hides everywhere."

His brother Ham shrugged his shoulders. "Why should we clean up? We won't be here much longer."

Noah smiled and nodded, pleased that Ham understood. "Leave the mess, Japheth," Noah said. "Let's enjoy the sight of our finished work."

Noah and his three sons set their eyes on the ark itself. Compared to the massive gopher wood structure, they looked tiny and frail. If they all stood on each other's shoulders, so that they were four-men tall, they would still reach barely halfway up the height of the ark. Shem had already remarked that running from one end of the ark to the other made him lose his breath.

The roof was covered in animal hides stretched across an enormous wooden frame. Tucked in just under the roof, a row of small windows would let in some fresh air. But they would not be able to see very much once they were inside the ark. The windows were too high up to look out without climbing up to them from the upper deck.

"It's not ugly," Noah said, smiling. "It's beautiful. Let's have a final look inside."

"Good," Shem said enthusiastically. "I was hoping you would say that." He turned to lead the way to the one and only door into the ark. The heavy, wide, wooden slab of a door swung down from its frame. When it was down, it formed a ramp. The four men walked up the ramp and entered the lower deck.

"We'll put the big animals down here." Noah reminded his sons of what they already knew. "Make sure that you distribute them evenly when we bring them in. We can't have them all at one end. We don't want to tip over in the first wind we face."

Noah's sons looked around the lower deck. They, too,

were pleased with what they saw. Above them were two more decks. Each of the three decks was divided into dozens of rooms. Noah and Shem had planned how all the animals would be arranged. The more dangerous animals would be separated from the peaceful ones. The wolves would be nowhere near the lambs. And the birds would need a safe place to fly, a spacious room with a high ceiling. Some of the rooms were very small. Others had dividing walls and shelves to help organize the smaller animals.

Some of the rooms would be used for storing food, both for the family and for the animals. Japheth had suggested having storage rooms at both ends of each deck so that they would not have to carry the heavy sacks of animal feed on their shoulders very far. The family would have a few small rooms for living space. It would not be as nice as the homes they had now, but they would make the rooms as comfortable as possible.

The four men walked the length of the lower deck, inspecting every room. Noah took note of the places that still needed to be cleaned or where the workmen had not done a satisfactory job. Everything must be perfect before they brought the animals in.

"Let's go upstairs," Noah said, leading the way to the middle deck.

The rooms looked large and wide while they were empty. Ham shook his head. "I can hardly believe we can ever fill up all this space, even with two of every living animal in the world."

"Don't forget," Shem added, "we have to have seven of every kind of bird."

Shem was in charge of collecting animals. His father turned to him for a report. "Are you finding all the animals we need, Shem?"

Shem nodded. "We've been working on getting the harder animals first. We can always find the common animals at the last minute, like rabbits and dogs and camels. We're right on schedule."

Japheth laughed. "We don't even know what the schedule is, do we, Father?"

Noah pressed his lips together thoughtfully. "No, I don't know the exact schedule. But it will not be long."

"Then we should begin loading supplies," Japheth said.

Noah nodded. "First thing in the morning. We'll start loading the food and supplies first. Do we have enough food gathered?"

It was Ham's turn to report. "It's hard to say if we have enough, since we don't know how long we'll be aboard."

"Father has already told us that the flood will last forty days and forty nights," Japheth said.

Ham nodded. "And then?"

"And then what?"

"And then how long will it be before we actually see dry land? And will there be anything left for us to eat when this is all over?"

"Ham is right," Shem agreed. "We have no idea what we will find when the flood is over."

"Or where we will be," Noah said. "Remember, we'll be afloat all that time."

"And when we do find dry land," Shem continued, "we'll have to start all over again. No laughing neighbors to help build anything. No cheating merchants to sell us their goods. It will be just the eight of us starting all over again."

For a long time, no one said anything. During the construction, they had focused on building the ark. While they gathered food and supplies, they had thought of what they needed while they were in the ark. How could they imagine what life would be like after the flood was over?

Noah sighed deeply. "We must obey the Lord. You have many questions, and I cannot answer them. I only know we must obey the Lord."

Walking more slowly, the foursome climbed the stairs to the upper deck. Even on the top deck, the walls rose far above their heads.

"Perhaps we should have made the windows bigger," Japheth suggested, "so we could see out."

"And we'll need plenty of fresh air once the ark is full of animals," Ham added.

Noah shook his head. "No. These are the instructions that God gave. Who are we to think we could design a better ark?"

His sons had no response.

"Okay, then," Japheth finally said, "in the morning we will begin loading hay and feed for the animals."

Noah nodded. "We must be ready."

CHAPTER 6

"Noah! We need a chicken for supper!" Noah's wife called from the fire where she stirred a pot.

Noah was standing among the chickens, feeding them.

"Well, my friends," he said, "I have to choose one of you. If I don't, she will."

Nine hens and three roosters clawed in the dirt. Furry yellow chicks chased after the bigger birds with tiny, quick steps. They all pecked furiously at the bits of grain that Noah tossed at them.

"You might as well have a good supper before you become supper," Noah murmured. He tossed out some more grain. The fattest hen of the bunch scurried over and filled her mouth greedily. Noah chuckled. "My wife would be very pleased if I brought you home."

Noah reached into his worn leather pouch for one more handful of grain. As he stretched out his arm to scatter it, he stopped. His fist tightened around the grain, and he stood perfectly still.

"This is a holy moment," he whispered to himself.

He was not sure how long he stood there before he moved again. Minutes? Hours? Finally he realized he was holding his breath and let it out.

"Seven days!" he exclaimed loudly.

"Father?" said a voice behind him. Noah spun around to see Shem watching him.

"Are you all right, Father?" Shem asked.

"Seven days," Noah repeated.

"Seven days?" Shem echoed.

"That's right. Seven days."

"Seven days for what, Father?"

Noah's eyes widened as he looked at Shem. "Until the flood begins, of course."

"The flood? Are you sure?" Excitement made Shem's voice rise.

Noah nodded vigorously. "I'm sure. The Lord just told me. We have seven days. We must be in the ark when the heavens open and the water begins."

"We can be ready," Shem assured his father.

"We have to be!"

"We just have to get organized," Shem continued. "The hay is ready. Ham started lining the stalls with it today."

"What about food for us?"

"Mother has a lot of meat hanging to dry. It should be ready. All the women have been grinding wheat, so we will have plenty of flour."

"Good. And what about the pairs?" Noah asked. "Do we have a male and female of every animal? That's the most important thing."

Shem shrugged. "A few of the animals are tricky. I have a few more to find."

"We have only seven days, Shem."

"It will be enough. If only I could find a female red fox, one of the small ones."

"But I saw a fox nearby today," Noah said. "I was afraid it was going to get the chickens, so I shooed it off."

"As long as the chickens are out, the fox will not be far off." Shem began to scan the yard.

"She went into the woods," Noah said, pointing.

"Then I'm going into the woods," Shem said with determination. He turned away from the chickens and toward the woods.

Suddenly, Noah grabbed his son's arm. "There she is," he whispered. "The fox—I see her eyes right over there." Two brown fox eyes peered out from the edge of the woods. They were fixed on the fat hen that Noah had chosen for supper.

Shem looked where his father pointed. "I see," he whispered. "Here I go."

Shem moved stealthily toward the edge of the wood. On his way, he picked up a length of rope. Smoothly but quickly, he moved across the yard, keeping his eyes fixed on the fox's eyes. He had been catching animals since he was a small boy. That was why Noah had given Shem the job of rounding up the animals. With one swift motion, he could snatch up the small animal and put a rope around its snout.

Noah held his breath as he watched his son. Shem had almost reached the fox. With the rope in one hand, Shem dove at the fox. Her tail brushed in his face as she scampered out of reach. Shem landed face down in the dirt. He groaned loudly.

Noah did not know whether to laugh or sigh. They needed that female fox, and he wanted Shem to catch her. But the sight of his determined son with his face in the dirt made him chuckle. Shem stood up, brushed himself off, and headed into the woods.

Noah turned back and crossed the yard toward his home. "Ham, Japheth," he called as he walked. "Get your wives. I need to talk to everyone."

No one answered. "Ham! Japheth! Get your wives!" Noah called again.

Finally the small group gathered, curious about what Noah had to say this time.

"The flood will begin in seven days," Noah announced. "We have seven days to prepare."

His wife scoffed. "Seven days! We have far too much to do. We cannot be ready in seven days. The vegetables will not be ready."

Noah laughed. "Do you think God is going to hold back the heavens because your vegetables are not ready?"

"Why didn't you tell me sooner?" his wife countered.

"I didn't know until just now," Noah answered. "We have one week. We must be ready." He turned and looked across the big yard. "I'm going to walk through the ark one last time. I want to be sure we are not forgetting anything."

"I'll tell you what you've forgotten," his wife said.

"You've forgotten our supper."

"Oh, yes, the chicken," Noah answered. "I have a hen picked out."

"We need that chicken in the pot soon."

"You'll have it," Noah assured his wife. He himself did not have much appetite. There was far too much to think about. He hardly wanted to take time to eat.

"I'll go with you, Father," Japheth offered. "We need to take a look at the upper deck. I think we need some more shelves in the stalls in the stern."

"Come along, then." Noah and Japheth started across the yard toward the ark.

"Where is Shem?" Japheth asked.

"Catching a fox," Noah answered.

Japheth chuckled. "The small female fox? He's been after one for weeks."

"Today is the day he'll catch her," Noah said, grinning. "He knows he's running out of time." He raised his eyes toward the woods. "There he is now."

Shem had indeed caught the fox. Her snout was muzzled with his rope, but she squirmed in his muscular arms. The look of determination on Shem's face told Noah that his son would not let the fox get away. However, Shem was covered in dirt, and his clothing was torn.

Japheth threw his head back and roared at the sight of his brother. "If you show up for supper looking like that, Mother will throw you in the pot instead of the chicken!"

Shem grinned in triumph. The small red fox thrashed in his arms.

"The pen is ready," Japheth said. "You'd better put her in with the others before she gets loose and grabs the chicken she's been after."

"The chicken!" Noah exclaimed. He whirled and scurried across the yard. "I must get the chicken!"

CHAPTER 7

"Are you sure that aardvark is female?" Japheth looked suspiciously at the scaly animal his brother had just penned up. "It looks just like the other one to me."

Shem sighed. He latched the gate to the pen. "I'm as sure as I can be," he answered.

"But what if you're wrong?" Japheth challenged. "If we don't have a pair to mate and breed, there won't be any more aardvarks when this is all over."

"Perhaps you would like to have a closer look," Shem suggested, "so you can see for yourself."

"Oh, I trust you," Japheth said quickly. "You're far more familiar with the animal species than I am."

Shem nodded. If Japheth trusted him, why was he asking questions about the aardvarks?

Everyone was tired. The seven days had passed too quickly. No one slept very much. Instead, they exhausted themselves day and night. Strings of dried meats and vegetables, mounds of hay and grain, cooking pots, firewood, clothing, bedding, tents, furniture—they had to take everything they could. Nothing would be left when they found dry land again.

And the animals! Shem had been rounding them up for weeks, but they kept coming. There were too many animals even for the large work yard. Shem had begun to move them inside. Hundreds were already in the ark.

From time to time, an animal they had never seen before turned up in the work yard outside the ark. They always showed up in pairs. When that happened, Shem added them to the list.

Sometimes he did not know what to call the strange creatures that appeared suddenly, so he made something up. In the last few days, he had gotten used to turning around and finding a male and female of some animal standing outside the ark. It was as if they were waiting to be told what to do. Birds, mammals, reptiles—Shem kept a careful account of everything he had. And he was sure he had a female aardvark. But maybe he could be more sure.

"I'll look again, Japheth," Shem said. He leaned on the fence and surveyed the pen of animals. "It can't hurt to double-check."

Japheth slapped his brother on the back. "Thanks, Shem. I know Father will appreciate the extra effort, too."

"Where is Father?" Shem asked.

"In the ark," Japheth answered. "Mother has some very particular ideas about how she wants the furniture arranged. Father and Ham are trying to make her happy."

Shem smiled and nodded.

"I hope she's happy with the cooking area," Japheth said. "We put it on the upper deck so the smoke will have somewhere to go. But the windows are small and very high."

"It will be fine, I'm sure," Shem said. "Mother will get used to it. We're all grateful to have the ark, considering what is coming." He lifted his eyes to the horizon.

Japheth followed his brother's gaze. The sky was heavy and gray. They had not seen the sun for nearly a week. Each day grew colder and more gloomy than the day before.

"Father says water will come from the sky and the ground," Shem said.

Japheth nodded. "It will last for forty days and forty nights. That's a lot of water!"

"It's hard to imagine what it will be like," Shem said softly. "We have only a few more hours."

"Then perhaps we'd better get started with the rest of these animals," Japheth suggested.

Shem nodded. "Let's start with that pen over there," he said, pointing.

"The big cats," Japheth said, scowling.

"Yes, the lions, the tigers, the panthers, the cheetahs, the leopards," Shem said. "But don't worry, Japheth. They have become very gentle the last few days. It's as if they understand that something incredible will happen. They will give us no trouble."

"What happened to the elephants and camels?" Japheth looked at an empty pen.

"I loaded them this morning," Shem answered. "They are in the lower level. We'll put the cats at the other end."

They began the parade of animals: The cats were followed

by the small furry animals, and after them came the amphibians. Shem had made a special tank for them so that they could have the water they needed, but also have a bit of indoor land. The birds came next—toucans and parakeets and parrots and blue jays and cardinals and robins and crows and swallows and doves and pelicans and wrens and pigeons and quail and ducks and swans. Then the ravens, eagles, falcons, black kites, horned owls, screech owls, great owls, gulls, hawks, ospreys, cormorants, storks, heron, hoopoe, and dozens of others.

"How do you keep them all straight?" Japheth asked as he ducked to avoid a swooping seagull.

Shem shrugged. "They all look different."

"I suppose you say the same thing about your bug collection."

Shem grinned. "Something like that." He had carefully sealed off space on the top deck for the insects. Fortunately, he could fit thousands of insects in a very small space: crickets and katydids, grasshoppers and bees, lady bugs and centipedes, spiders by the dozens, butterflies by the hundreds. Some of the bugs he had never seen before; they just appeared in the room. He stopped trying to count them.

After checking on the monkeys and apes and the oxen and goats on the middle deck, Shem and Japheth went back outside. They planned to bring in the cattle and sheep next. They did not expect to see what they saw.

Japheth's eyes grew wide. "They've all lined up, Shem!"

He looked at the lines of animals. The animal pens were open, and the animals were lined up in pairs: gerbils and guinea pigs, hamsters and rabbits, zebras, hippos, and rhinoceroses, black bears, brown bears, raccoons, skunks, squirrels, llamas, bighorn sheep. The line seemed like it would never end.

"Shem, where did you find all these animals?" Japheth asked.

Shem was so surprised himself that he could hardly breathe. "I didn't," he said. "I found a few of them, but some of them I've never seen before. I don't even know what to call them."

Stunned, the two brothers watched as the animals paraded toward the ark: kangaroos, pandas, penguins, ostriches, tortoises, bison, deer, gazelles, ibex, antelope.

Japheth laughed. "Even if we don't know what to call them, they're coming with us."

"Two of every kind of animal," Shem said. "That's what God told Father. I guess He didn't mean just the ones I knew."

Noah appeared in the doorway of the ark. A panda was curious about him and swatted at him. Noah ducked away from the great paw.

"Shem, what is that?" Noah called out. He moved to the side of the ramp so that the parade of animals could continue. "How do they all know what to do?"

Shem shrugged. "It's out of my hands now, Father. I think we're just supposed to wait."

"They'd better stay out of Mother's kitchen," Japheth said, "or she'll fix one of them for supper."

Noah laughed. "Somehow I think they'll end up just where they should be. The two of you should come aboard, too."

Shem and Japheth followed their father back up the ramp and into the ark.

Noah glanced at the darkening sky. "It won't be long now."

CHAPTER 8

"Are we all here?" Noah asked, looking around the small kitchen his wife had organized. Large cooking pots hung on hooks above his head. He reminded himself that he would have to duck every time he walked through the kitchen.

"Four men, four wives," his wife answered. "We are all here."

"Shem, have the animals finished loading?"

"I think so," Shem answered, nodding. "For awhile, new ones kept showing up every few minutes, but I think they've stopped coming. There haven't been any new ones for several hours."

"Then it's time to close the door," Noah answered somberly. "Ham, you come with me, and we'll close the door."

Together, father and son made their way down to the lower deck to the only door the ark had. They were ready to pull on the long, thick ropes and heave the heavy door up and closed. Then they would cover it with pitch to seal out the water.

"Father, look!" Ham said as they approached the door. He stopped in his tracks and pointed.

Noah nodded slowly. "The door is already sealed. God has closed it Himself."

"Then there is nothing for us to do."

"That's right. God has done it all. Let's go back to the others."

On the upper deck once again, the eight members of the family sat in a close circle. The air was chilly even inside the ark.

"Now what?" someone asked.

"Now the rain," Noah answered.

They sat in silence for a long time.

"Will it come soon?" one of the wives asked.

Noah nodded.

Silence came once again. Then the dripping sound started. Pitter, pitter, patter. Pitter, patter.

Ham raised his eyes to the high row of small windows above them. "I wish we could see out."

Noah shook his head. "There is no need to see out. What God is doing for us, He will do inside here."

"It's growing dark," Noah's wife said. "Perhaps we should light a lamp."

Noah nodded. The rain was falling steadily. The ground was parched with thirst and would soak up the waters eagerly at first. The ark was huge and heavy with the weight of the animals. Noah knew it might be days before they would feel the ark lift and begin to float. More days would pass before the neighbors who had made fun of him would know that Noah had been right after all. The rains were not going to stop, not for forty days and forty nights.

Outside, the sky cracked open with a bolt of lightning.

Inside, everyone jumped at the sound. Thunder roared and rattled the vessel. Water poured from the heavens and struck the ark with a force that rocked it. Noah caught hold of a table to balance himself.

"Everyone sit down and hold on to each other," Noah called out above the thunder.

With a great groan, the earth beneath them split, and water gushed out of the great crack and swirled ferociously around the ark.

"What was that?" Shem's wife asked anxiously.

"The springs of the great deep have burst forth," Noah told her. "Everything is happening just the way God said it would."

The ground under them creaked open wider. The family huddled around one small lamp for the longest time. The storm raged around them. The air coming in the high row of windows was damp and cold, but the overhanging roof kept out the water. Inside, the family was dry and safe.

"The animals will need to be fed," Noah said a few hours later.

Shem swallowed hard. "I guess we'll find out now whether our system is going to work. Ham, Japheth, come with me. I'll show you what to do."

Two days passed. Tending to the animals kept all eight members of the family busy. Feeding them, bringing fresh rain water to drink, and cleaning out the stalls was tedious work. But there was little else to do for the next forty days, so they worked side by side and kept up with the chores. Noah's wife kept a small fire burning in the kitchen for warmth and cooking.

On the third day, Shem and Noah were feeding the small animals on the upper deck.

"What was that?" Shem asked suddenly. He tilted his head to listen for the sound once more. The raging storm made it hard to hear anything. He put down his bag of nuts and moved to the wall of the ark. Turning his ear to the wall, he listened again. "There it is again!"

"Noah!" came a faint voice. "You were right. Let us in!"

"Did you hear that?" Shem asked his father.

Noah hung his head. "The neighbors," he said softly.

"What should we do?" Shem asked. "Shall we make room for a few more?"

Noah shook his head sadly. "No, we cannot do that. God said only the eight of us would survive."

Shem opened his mouth to say something, then closed it. What could he say? His father was right. As the rumor spread about the ark project, hundreds of people had heard about it. And they had all laughed, every single one of them. No one believed what Noah said. No one believed in God. Besides, the door to the ark had been sealed, and the windows were too small and too high for anyone to crawl through.

The cries from outside came again, pleading to be allowed to enter.

"How long will they stay out there?" Shem wondered aloud.

Noah shrugged. "They will soon leave us and look for higher ground."

"I feel sorry for them, Father. Am I wrong to feel sorry for people whom God wants to punish?"

Noah shook his head. "You have a tender heart, Shem, a compassionate heart. It's not easy to listen to their cries. But we built this ark and loaded all the animals because we believed God and wanted to obey Him. We cannot change our minds now."

"You're right, of course," Shem answered his father. Sadly, he picked up his bag of animal food. Just then lightning split the sky once more, and the storm grew even louder. Shem could no longer hear the cries of his neighbors. He tossed a handful of nuts at the squirrels.

"Do these animals never sleep?" Noah asked as he stared at a raccoon. "They're always hungry."

The male squirrel scampered up the wall of the room and perched on a high shelf. Soon the female joined him. Holding a nut in her tiny hands, she gnawed on it.

"I never knew how much rabbits could eat," Shem said. "We only brought two rabbits aboard, but I have a feeling we'll have quite a few more before this journey is over."

Noah laughed. "We'll have more of a lot of things. But that's what God wants. The animals are supposed to multiply when we find dry land again. Some of them are just getting a head start."

The sky cracked open once more. Neither Shem nor Noah flinched this time. After listening to the earsplitting thunder for three days, they were all used to it. The rumbling of the skies never seemed to fade away completely. Wherever they were inside the ark, they could hear the storm raging outside. The water poured down in steady, heavy sheets of rain. Everything was damp all the time. But there was no point in complaining, so no one did. After all, this was only the beginning.

CHAPTER 9

The days passed slowly. But every once in a while, something exciting happened. Noah and his wife were standing in the little kitchen when they felt the ark lift and pitch slightly to one side. Others felt it, too. Their sons came running down the wide, wooden hallway of the upper deck, and their wives dashed in from their work cleaning stalls. They all stood together as they felt the vessel lift off the ground and begin to float. The ark began to sway gently in the rising water.

"Now our journey truly begins," Noah said.

"And we find out if those workmen were worth what we paid them," Japheth remarked.

They inspected the ark from stern to bow and side to side. They found no leaks. The vessel was sturdy and well constructed.

Gradually, they got used to the motion of rocking in the water. They learned how to walk without losing their balance. Japheth and Ham tied down any supplies that might slide across the decks.

First one week went by, then the second one and the third. Noah and his family fell into a routine of tending the animals. Shem's system for feeding and cleaning seemed to be working. No area of the ark was neglected. The right kinds of food for the animals on each deck were stored in places that were easy to get to. Each day's schedule called for certain animal stalls to be cleaned. The job was a big one. Thousands of animals kept them busy every minute of the day.

When they were not working, the family enjoyed eating their meals together. They had only each other for conversation. They told each other everything they did and everything they observed.

"The monkeys are starting to smell," Ham said one day, scrunching up his nose. "We'll have to clean their stalls more often."

Shem nodded. "I agree. I will change the schedule."

"We should throw some rain water at them," Japheth's wife suggested. "They need a bath."

"We can get all the rain water we need," Ham said confidently. He had rigged up a system to set out a basket on the upper deck and pull it in through one of the windows when it was full of water. A tall ladder allowed Ham and his brothers to climb up to the corner window and peek out under the edge of the roof. They could not see very much, but at least they could get water whenever they needed it.

"I didn't know the birds would be so noisy!" Shem said. "When they are outside, their little noises are soothing and pleasant. But when they are cooped up inside and all together in one place, the racket is not so nice."

"And the woodpecker!" Japheth added. "He's going to peck right through the wall one of these days. It echoes up and down the decks. He makes so much noise, and he pecks all day long. I wish he would be more quiet."

"He is simply doing what God created him to do," Noah said, chuckling. "A woodpecker must peck wood."

"Does he have to do it all the time?" Japheth asked.

Noah laughed. "It is a nuisance. But the day will come when we leave the ark, and you'll be sorry to see him go."

Japheth looked doubtful. He did not care if he ever saw another woodpecker.

"I've lost count of the days," Shem said. "Is this day twenty-five or twenty-six?"

"Actually, this is day twenty-seven," Japheth informed him. "I've been marking the days off by scratching on the wall on the middle deck."

Ham laughed. "It looks like the woodpecker is not the only thing pecking wood."

Even Japheth smiled at that. "At least my scratchings have a purpose. And I don't keep anyone awake at night by doing it."

"Day twenty-seven," Shem repeated thoughtfully, "and it is going to rain for forty days. We're more than halfway through."

Japheth shook his head. "This is only the beginning. It will be weeks, maybe even months, before we find dry land."

"Do you really think it will take that long for the water to run off?" Shem asked.

His brother nodded. "There is nowhere for the water to go. By now the earth must be soaked very deeply. It will take a long time to dry out."

"We must be sure the land is safe for the animals," Noah reminded his sons. "They share the job of rebuilding the earth."

"We have a long wait ahead of us," Japheth insisted.

"Well, we have plenty of supplies," Ham said, "and the smaller animals are already breeding, so we'll have chickens and rabbits to eat."

Shem turned to his father. "Where do you think we will end up, Father?"

Noah smiled slightly. "We will end up exactly where God wants us to be."

"But where will that be?" Shem pressed. "Will we be anywhere near our home?"

Japheth jumped in. "I don't think so, Shem. The waters are rising fast and moving fast. We are not staying in one place. We are floating farther from home every day."

"It won't matter," Ham said. "There will be nothing left at home anyway. We're all that's left by now."

No one spoke for a long time after that. It was hard to imagine leaving the ark and finding no one else alive.

The rain came steadily. On some days, the sky broke open with a storm, and the wind swept the ark in circles. Lightning cracked the night, and thunder rumbled from one end of the ark to the other. On other days, the rain was calmer. But it was always heavy. And it never stopped. Whether they were sleeping, eating, feeding the animals, or talking to each other, the eight people in the ark always heard the sound of the rain in the background. During a storm, they simply raised their voices so others could hear them.

Noah found time to be by himself. Each evening, after the chores were done for the day, and the rest of the family had found their beds, he walked to the other end of the upper deck. The eyes of the animals watched him in the dark, until he came to his favorite spot. There he would listen to the rain. And some nights he would hear the voice of God in the storm. He would stay and listen for God to speak in the rain until he was again full of assurance that God was taking care of him and his family. Then Noah would return to his mat on the floor next to his wife and sleep peacefully, no matter how much thunder rumbled outside.

CHAPTER 10

Japheth let his fingers slide gently over his markings in the hall of the middle deck. He counted softly under his breath, just to make sure. He counted thirty-seven marks. For thirty-seven days, the rain had deluged the earth. For thirty-seven days, the animals had cheeped and growled and chirped. For thirty-seven days, they tooted and thumped and quacked. They baaed, hissed, and gobbled. They woofed, meowed, mooed, and cuckooed. And the woodpecker pecked wood. For thirty-seven days, the woodpecker pecked. For thirty-seven days, Japheth wished the woodpecker would stop pecking wood.

Noah came out of the stall where the goats and bighorn sheep were. He was careful to close the gate securely behind him. The last thing he needed was for any of the animals to get loose and stir up chaos on the decks of the ark.

Noah walked slowly over to where Japheth stood. "Day thirty-seven," he said.

Japheth rubbed the wall. "That's right, day thirty-seven."

"Three more days, then," Noah said, "and the change will come."

Japheth grinned at his father. "I'd like to know if the change will make the woodpecker stop pecking wood."

Noah laughed. "I told Ham to put an extra post in the aviary."

"Father, you're just encouraging the woodpecker to keep going."

"It's better if he pecks at a post than if he knocks a hole in the wall."

"I suppose you're right."

The animals did not know the difference as day thirty-seven became day thirty-eight and then day thirty-nine. But the family's excitement grew. Noah's wife suddenly had the urge to straighten up the living quarters and scrub them till they were spotless. Shem strolled the decks with his wife, humming cheerful melodies. Ham made a fresh list of the supplies they had left.

When Japheth woke on day forty, he heard the same steady background sound that he had heard for the thirty-nine days before. Wind swirled around the ark, and the water came down in sheets. At first, he wanted to find his father and ask a hundred questions. But he didn't. He just reminded himself that God had said it would rain for forty days and forty nights. One more day. That night would be the fortieth night. Surely in the morning, the rain would stop, Japheth told himself.

When Japheth woke on day forty-one, he again heard the gray, dull sound of the rain. He went to find his father. Noah was standing on the top deck, with his eyes raised to the high windows.

"This is the day, isn't it, Father?" Japheth asked.

Noah nodded.

Shem appeared on the deck. Soon Ham joined them, too. And then the women came. All eight of them stood in a small clear area on the top deck. They were in the corner where Ham had rigged a ladder. No one spoke very much. What was there to say? They were waiting for the rain to stop. It was the only thing that mattered right then. They watched the small windows for any sign of change in the weather.

After a long time, Noah's wife said, "I suppose I might as well go fix lunch. This day sounds like every other day."

Noah shook his head. "No. Today will be different."

"So far, it is the same, old man," his wife answered. She shuffled across the deck. "Waiting makes me hungry. I'm going to go make soup."

Her feet scraped along the wooden floor, making the planks squeak. But Noah was not listening to his wife's shuffling. He was hearing a different sound.

"There!" Noah cried. "The wind has stopped. It is not howling. The air is still for the first time in forty days."

Everyone stood perfectly still, including Noah's wife. They tilted their heads and listened.

"And the rain has stopped," Noah continued. "I hear only the water lapping up against the side of the ark. But I don't hear rain."

Shem pointed at a window. "Look, sunlight! The sun is coming out!"

Seven other heads turned to the high corner window.

The roof of the ark, made out of leather hides, hung over the window and cast a thin shadow. But the air around the window was definitely filled with light.

"I want to see!" Ham blurted out, and he scrambled up the ladder he had built in the corner.

"Hurry," his mother said. "Tell us what you see."

Ham reached the top swiftly. He hoisted himself up and stretched his neck out as far as he could.

"All I see is water," he called back to the others.

"Forty days of rain, and he expects to see land?" Japheth said, laughing.

"I see more water than I could ever imagine," Ham said. "It's an ocean out there. We're floating in the middle of an ocean!" He pulled himself back inside the ark and turned to his brothers. "I knew the flood waters would cover the earth," he said, "but I just never imagined what it would look like. It will be months before we see land again."

"But the sun is shining, right?" Shem asked.

Ham nodded. "Yes, the sun is shining—very brightly. There's not a cloud in the sky."

Noah nodded with satisfaction. "Of course the sun is shining. Of course there are no clouds. God said the flood would stop after forty days. Did any of you doubt that the sun would shine again?"

His sons shook their heads.

"Of course we knew the sun would shine," Japheth said, "but it still feels good to see it."

The others nodded. Even Noah had to agree that the sunlight was welcome.

"Now do you want some lunch?" Noah's wife asked the rest of the family.

"We'll help you," her daughters-in-law said.

"I'm so excited, I could eat a cow," Japheth said.

"Don't even think about it," Noah said, laughing. "We won't slaughter any animals until they have a chance to breed properly."

"I have some special cakes," Noah's wife said. "We'll have them with our soup for a celebration."

Noah's wife, his sons, and their wives moved toward the other end of the upper deck, where their living quarters were. Noah watched all seven of them walk away.

"Thank You, Lord, for sparing my family," he said softly. "We are safe in Your care. If it rained another forty days and forty nights, we would still be safe in Your care."

When his family was out of sight, Noah sighed with satisfaction. He knew that in only a few minutes his wife would call him to lunch. But for now, he only wanted to look up at the window one more time and see the beam of light that seemed to fall right on his face.

CHAPTER 11

The woodpecker's beady little eyes glared at Japheth. Japheth's dark brown eyes stared back at the bird. In his mind he dared the little creature to go back to drilling his way through a log hung on a hook in his cage. The bird had been quiet for the last few days, and Japheth wanted things to stay that way. He tossed an extra handful of grain on the floor of the cage. Perhaps the woodpecker would want to eat and forget about pecking.

The din of the animals got on Japheth's nerves. The elephants screeched, the ducks honked, the lions roared, the beavers buzzed, the hippos sloshed around in their indoor mud. The tigers snarled, the pigs oinked and snorted, the camels brayed, the horses neighed, the cows mooed, the birds flapped and twittered. The crickets chirped, the bees buzzed, the monkeys chattered. And the woodpecker pecked wood.

During the weeks of rain, Japheth's head had been filled with the sounds of the raging storm. Now he heard animals every minute of the day, every day of the week. His head rang with noise, and there was nowhere to go to escape it. Sometimes he just wanted a bit of peace and quiet. How long would it take for the earth to dry up so that they could leave the ark?

The woodpecker ignored Japheth's offering of extra grain. The little eyes stayed fixed on Japheth.

"Have it your way," Japheth said aloud. "Eat, or don't eat. It doesn't matter to me." He turned to move on up the deck to the next set of animals waiting for their dinner.

Suddenly a roar of air drowned out all of the animal noises. Japheth dropped his feed bag and put his hands over his ears. Never in his life had he heard such a sound. It was like a wind—but much greater than even the fiercest wind during the weeks of rain. *Will there be another storm?* Japheth wondered. Would the rains return and batter them once more? "Father!" Japheth called out. Leaving his grain bag behind, he began to walk up the main aisle, looking for his father.

The ark rocked violently from side to side. Japheth tumbled to the floor. He tried to scramble to his feet again, but instead, he slid backward. The front of the ark was raised much higher than the rear. The animals screamed in protest as they were thrown against the walls of their stalls and cages. Japheth heard the thud, thud, thud as the larger animals hit the walls.

"Father!" Japheth called again. Once again he tried to stand up. With both hands, he grasped the railing that ran along the wall. "Father!" One slow step at a time, Japheth pulled himself along the aisle. He had left his father at the other end of the deck, cleaning out the zebra stalls.

The roar grew louder. Japheth could hardly hear his own thoughts. The ark tipped dangerously. Suddenly Japheth wanted to know where everyone was—Shem and Ham and their wives, as well as his own wife and both his parents. Surely the storm was starting again. What other explanation could there be? Any minute now, he would heard the sound of the water striking the leather roof of the ark, as it had for forty days and forty nights.

In determination, Japheth kept moving. "Father! Father!" The ark rocked from left to right, and Japheth lost his grip on the railing. He tumbled to the floor once more. He got back on his feet as quickly as he could. The howling roar drowned out everything around him.

At last, Japheth caught a glimpse of his father moving toward him. They met in the middle of the aisle and embraced.

"Father, what's happening?" Japheth asked anxiously. "The rain has been over for months. Why is it storming again?"

Noah shook his head. "There is no storm."

"But the wind, Father!" Japheth said. "What else could it be? The rain this time will be worse than before."

Again Noah shook his head. "There is no storm," he repeated. "There will be no more rain."

"Then tell me what this sound is," Japheth demanded.

"I don't know," Noah admitted. "But it cannot be more rain. God said the rain would stop after forty days and forty nights. And it did stop. God has kept us safe so far, and He will keep us safe until the flood is over."

"We must find out what this wind means," Japheth said. "Come with me to the upper deck. I'll climb the ladder and look out the window."

The wind howled, and the ark pitched from side to side. Slowly, one step at a time, Noah and Japheth made their way to the upper deck and stumbled to the corner where the ladder hung beneath the window.

Shem was already halfway up the ladder. Ham and the women had gathered as well.

"Come down, Shem," Noah commanded.

"But we must see what is happening," Shem insisted. He climbed a rung higher on the ladder.

"Come down!" Noah repeated. "I will go up and look out the window."

"But, Father," Shem protested, "it will be faster if I—"

Noah waved his hand to say that his son should be silent and obey. Reluctantly, Shem lowered himself rung by rung until he stood on the deck with everyone else.

Noah grasped the sides of the ladder and put his foot on the first rung. He moved steadily but slowly. On the fourth rung, his foot slipped. The whole family gasped. Shem loudly insisted his father should come down, but Noah ignored him. Noah caught his balance, steadied himself, and began to climb again. He conquered ten rungs, then fifteen, then twenty. Finally he reached the window.

Standing on the top rung of the ladder, Noah pushed his hands on the bottom of the small window and pulled himself up. The opening was barely big enough to put his head through. He knew he would never get his shoulders through.

He looked out, past the eaves of the roof, past the edges of the ark, to the water. What he saw made him tighten his grip on the window sill.

"What do you see, Father?" his sons called out. "Tell us what you see."

"God is rolling back the water," Noah answered. "He has sent the wind of His Spirit to push back the water."

"Can you see land?" everyone wanted to know.

CHAPTER 12

Noah did not see land. But he firmly believed they would see land soon. Just as God had brought the waters, now He would push them away. But there was a lot of water. It might take a very long time.

On the deck below him, his family clung to the walls and railings to keep their balance. Carefully, slowly, Noah lowered himself down the ladder and joined them.

"We can go back to our chores," he told the huddled group. He had to shout to be heard above the wind.

"Just go back to work?" Ham asked, also shouting. "Like nothing is happening?"

"The animals must be fed. Their stalls must be cleaned," Noah insisted. "I should be finished with the zebras soon."

Japheth began to nod his head slowly. "What you mean, Father, is that you do not know how long this will last. We must carry on with our responsibilities while we wait."

Noah nodded. "That is what I mean. It could be weeks before the water is gone. Go finish feeding the birds. Shem, the big animals may need some new drinking water. I would imagine a lot of the troughs have spilled." Noah ignored his family's stares as he moved past them and began to make his way back to the zebras. He did not look back or say anything more. Slowly, the others followed him back to work.

For days, weeks, months, the family carried on this way. They could hear the wind and knew that the waters were drying up. The ark rocked from side to side. They felt the motion of the swirling water. But how long would it be before they found land?

Then, one day, the ark stopped. The wind stopped. The waters stopped rolling. The ark no longer pitched from side to side. When the hippos and the rhinos and the elephants all moved to one side of the ark, the vessel still stayed flat. Even the woodpecker seemed to sense a change and stopped pecking wood.

Once again, Noah's three sons scrambled to the ladder to see what was happening. And once again, he called them down and insisted on climbing the rungs himself. The anxious family stood below him, waiting for his announcement.

"We are indeed stopped," he shouted, as he looked out the window. "We seem to be on top of a mountain."

"Is there dry land?" Shem asked. "Can you see any land at all?"

Noah scanned the horizon. His view from the small window was limited. But everywhere he looked he saw water. No treetops, no fields, just water. It was as if they were an island in the middle of a vast, unending lake. The blue of the water met the blue of the sky so perfectly that Noah could hardly tell where the water ended and the sky began. As beautiful as it was, he had hoped for something else.

He turned to his family and shook his head. No land,

except the very tip of the mountain on which they sat.

So they waited some more. They had already been in the ark for half a year. Japheth had filled a large patch of wall with his scratchings to count the days. Shem and Ham would often go down and recount the marks, as if they could speed the time by finding some mistake in Japheth's arithmetic.

Some of the family were getting restless. They gazed up at the windows, longing to run free and feel the rush of fresh air on their faces. But, as Noah liked to remind his family, where else did they have to go? So they waited. Every day, someone climbed the ladder and studied the view. They looked for any spot of brown, a tree trunk, perhaps, or the dirt on the side of the mountain. They looked for anything green, perhaps the budding leaf on a branch or the lush, thick grass of a meadow. For three months, they watched and waited.

Finally, the day came that Noah announced he could see the tops of several other mountains below them. Wherever they were, they were very high.

"We're sitting on top of the world," Shem marveled as he looked out one day. He could see nothing around them that was higher than they were.

After they saw the tops of the mountains, Noah began to count the days again. He waited forty days. And then one morning, he said, "Shem, bring me a raven."

With the bird on his shoulder and his family standing on the upper deck, Noah climbed the ladder. At the top, he grasped the bird with both hands, whispered a prayer for its safety, and tossed it out the window. The black wings opened immediately and began to flap. Noah smiled as the shiny black bird soared against the blue sky. *God made birds for flying,* he told himself, *not for being cooped up within the walls of an ark.*

The raven flew back and forth, back and forth. Noah watched it pass the window each time. He turned to his family and shook his head. The raven could find no good place to land.

They waited again. They fed the animals, cleaned the stalls, and tried not to think about how the raven had circled the ark with nowhere else to go.

Then Noah climbed the ladder once more, this time with a dove in his hands. Perhaps by now there would be a tree-top where a bird might find a home. He tossed it out the window. Its wings fluttered open, and the dove began to circle. Its shimmering white color was almost lost in the bright sunlight, but Noah kept his eyes fixed on it. It flew east and west; it flew north and south. It circled widely around the ark. But in the end, it came back to Noah at the window. Noah reached out his arm, and the dove gently landed on his hand. The old man pulled it to safety within the upper deck of the ark.

Noah stood at the top of the ladder, with his family waiting below, and stroked the soft feathers of the dove. "Perhaps a few more days," he said softly. "We'll try again in a few more days. You will be the one to tell us about our new home."

He could see the disappointment in the faces of his family. But they had no choice. They would have to wait some more.

CHAPTER 13

Seven days later, Noah climbed the ladder with the dove once again. The instant he opened his hand, the bird fluttered its wings and lifted off into the free air. Noah hunched through the window as far as he could to watch where the bird went. Would it circle and come back? Or would it find its freedom in a new life?

The bird was soon out of sight. Noah's heart beat a little faster. The bird did not come back right away as it had the week before, or as the raven had the week before that.

Looking around from the mountaintop perch, Noah could see that the water around them had gone down. Patches of land had appeared on the mountainsides. It was difficult to see anything from the tiny window tucked under the eaves of the ark's roof, but what Noah saw made him hopeful. But they were so high up. They would have to find land at a lower elevation, or there would be no hope of growing food. The family had lived inside the ark among the animals for eleven months. Even Noah, who was more patient than all the others, was ready to get out. He longed to walk on solid ground, to eat fresh vegetables, to pray with his face lifted to the sun.

Noah looked for the dove again. It was nowhere in sight.

"Father, aren't you coming down?" Shem asked.

Noah shook his head. "I'm going to wait for the dove."

"Hasn't it come back?" Shem asked, with a hint of excitement in his voice.

"No, but it may still come back."

"You'll get tired sitting up on top of the ladder."

"I'll be fine, Shem."

"Mother will not approve."

"No, she won't."

Noah just could not bring himself to leave his watching place. Every minute that the dove stayed out of sight gave him more hope.

The day passed slowly, but at last evening came. Noah's eyes darted around the horizon, looking for the dove. Had it found a treetop where it could build a nest? Had it found enough leaves and branches to use for a nest?

And then the bird came back. It landed softly on Noah's arm. For a moment, Noah's heart sank. He had truly hoped that the bird would not come back this time. And then, Noah looked more closely. The dove's beak was clamped shut around something green.

Noah reached for the bird and pried open its beak.

"It's a leaf!" he called down to his family. He started to climb down the ladder. "It's an olive leaf!"

"An olive leaf?" Japheth echoed. "But olive trees do not grow on the tops of mountains. They grow much lower down."

Noah nodded excitedly. "That's right. This little dove has been all the way down the side of the mountain, and he's come back to tell us that the waters are nearly gone."

"Can we leave the ark, then?" Ham asked.

Noah shook his head. "Not yet. We'll wait a few more days. Then we'll send the dove out again. If he doesn't come back, then we'll know the time is right."

So they waited some more. Seven days crawled by. Japheth marked off seven more scratches on his wall. Shem and Ham nervously tried to concentrate on their chores.

Finally Noah climbed the ladder again with the dove and shooed it out the window. Then he settled on the top of the ladder to wait. The family gathered below. They waited all day and long into the evening. The bird did not come back. The family hardly slept that night. They knew what the dove's absence meant. They knew what the morning would bring. Everyone was up before dawn.

Shem scrambled up the ladder and looked around for the dove. Grinning, he looked down at his anxious family and shook his head. The dove had not returned!

"Throw off the roof," Noah commanded.

His sons needed no further prompting. They shinnied up the walls and tugged at the hides sewn together for the roof. Their muscles rippled as they pulled the hides apart at the seams. Eagerly and joyfully, they rolled the roof back. Sunlight bathed the upper deck of the ark. People and animals alike squinted at the brightness.

"It looks dry, Father!" Japheth called out. He stood at the railing of the ark, looking over the side and studying the ground forty-five feet below him.

Noah nodded, his own excitement shining in his eyes.

"Let's go!" Shem cried. "Come on, Ham, let's open the door on the lower deck." Ham quickly fell into step with Shem, and they ran across the deck to the stairs.

"Wait!" Noah called after his sons. "Not yet."

They stopped and turned to look at him. "The ground is dry, Father. You can see that for yourself."

"I know," Noah answered, "and I want to get off the ark as much as you do. But God has not yet said it is time."

"What do you mean? Are we going to stay here? Keep waiting?"

Noah nodded at his doubtful sons. "That is what we will do."

"But the animals, Father," Shem protested. "It's time for them to move about freely."

"And for us to do the same!" Japheth added.

"We will wait," Noah said simply.

So they waited. Weeks went by. Japheth scratched off the days. Soon they reached the one-year mark—one year of living inside the ark with the animals.

Noah woke early one morning. As soon as his eyes popped open, he knew he must go down to the lower deck and check the door. As he moved through the aisles on the lower deck, he felt the rush of fresh air. Just as he suspected, the door was open.

"Come out of the ark," a voice said. "You and your wife and your sons and their wives. Bring out every kind of living creature that is with you—the birds, the animals, and all the creatures that move along the ground—so that they can multiply on the earth and be fruitful and increase in number upon it."

Noah strode through the aisles of the decks and threw open the latches on the stalls and catches. He pulled the doors and gates open. He thumped the rumps of the bigger animals to get them moving. By the time he got to the small monkeys, Shem had discovered what he was doing. Within a few minutes, the whole family was there, shooing animals out of the ark and into the daylight—and onto solid ground.

Some animals went eagerly. Some were not so sure. But with prodding from Noah and his family, they spilled out of the ark and onto the land. The woodpecker whizzed by Japheth's head and disappeared into a thicket of trees.

Japheth roared with laughter. Shem shrieked with delight. Ham whooped with joy. Noah raised his face and smiled at heaven.

CHAPTER 14

Shem rolled in the grass until he was covered in dirt and dew. Ham climbed the tallest tree he could find. Japheth decided that he enjoyed the sound of the woodpecker—in the forest. The women rushed to pick wildflowers blooming on the mountainside and searched for the fresh herbs that had been missing from their food for the last year.

The animals kept coming from the ark. They poured out onto the side of the mountain, squinted in the sunlight, and began their new lives. The birds soared in the sky, swirling and swooping before disappearing from sight. The panthers and cheetahs and other animals that were made for fleet running were gone in an instant. Once the grand exit began, no human or animal wanted it to end.

Noah watched it all. Like the rest of his family, he was eager to stand on firm ground again. But he was too old to roll in the grass or climb a tree. He stood outside the ark and watched the excitement around him.

"Where will all the animals go?" Shem asked. "So many of them appeared out of nowhere last year. What if they can't survive around here?"

Noah smiled knowingly. "God will take them back to where they belong."

"So we won't see them again?"

"Perhaps not."

Shem scowled. "I got used to having them around. I'll miss them."

"So will I," said Japheth, as he came up behind them.

"Even the woodpecker?" Noah asked, laughing.

"Oh, maybe even the woodpecker!"

Noah raised his hands above his head. "We must thank God for keeping us safe, as well as all the animals—even the woodpecker. Japheth, bring me some stones and some wood. Shem, I'll need some birds for a sacrifice."

"Now I understand why we needed seven of some of the birds," Shem said. "It's so that there will be some to sacrifice and others to breed and multiply."

"That's exactly right," Noah answered. "Let's get busy with this altar."

Soon the whole family was helping to build the altar. The stones were in place, and the fire lit. Noah prepared the birds.

"This is an offering of thanksgiving and dedication," Noah explained. "We will express our gratitude for God's safekeeping for the last year. Then we will dedicate ourselves to serve Him for the rest of our lives."

The family watched solemnly as Noah sacrificed the birds.

"Listen," Noah said to his family, "and you will hear God speak."

The wind swirled around them, and the smoke from the sacrifice floated upward. And they did hear God speak. The only eight people on earth stood and listened as the God Who cared for them spoke. No one moved a muscle.

"That was a holy moment," Noah said, when it was over. "You must never forget it."

"How could we forget it?" Japheth asked. "We have survived the flood that destroyed the whole earth, and now God has promised that He will never again destroy all living creatures because people are sinful."

"We are still sinful," Noah warned his family. "Just because we have been spared from the flood, we must not think that we are perfect. We are all capable of the cruel and thoughtless things that we saw others do. God has promised not to destroy the earth again because of our sin. But we must never forget that we are sinners."

Noah turned away from the altar and opened his arms wide. "We have a whole new world," he said. "God has made a covenant with me, a promise. And He makes it with you, because you are my descendants. And you will have descendants of your own. You must never forget. And you can be sure that God will never forget what He has promised."

"Look!" Shem cried. "In the sky, over there!"

Seven pairs of eyes turned to see what Shem had seen. A band of light, shining with every color they could imagine, bent over the horizon. It sparkled in the sunlight and reflected majestically in the pools and ponds that dotted the mountainside. It disappeared over the horizon and then circled back and surrounded them.

"It's beautiful!" Noah's wife exclaimed.

"It's a rainbow," Noah explained. "The rainbow is God's sign that He will keep His promise. Whenever it appears in the sky, God will remember His promise.

"And so will we," Shem said.

"Yes," Noah agreed. "And so will we."

Joseph

Slave Turned Ruler

by Rex Williams

CHAPTER 1

Many hundreds of years ago, in a far-off land named
Canaan, a boy named Joseph lived with his father and
eleven brothers. Joseph was a lot like you and me in many
ways—he liked to run, to play in the fields, to sit and talk or
play games with his brothers, and he enjoyed a good meal
as well as anyone. But there was one thing Joseph had that
made a big difference in his life and in the lives of many
other people: Joseph had great faith in God. Joseph believed
with all his heart that God was able to see him through any
trouble no matter how bad it might seem. He knew that God
cared about him and would always be there when he called
out to Him for help. God did allow Joseph to face many
tough situations in his lifetime, but God was always there to
help him out of them. This is the story of Joseph.

Now Joseph's father, Jacob, loved Joseph more than his
other sons, because Joseph had been born when Jacob was
an old man. When Joseph's brothers saw that Jacob loved
Joseph more than them, they were no longer nice to their
brother. They barely spoke to him at all, and when they did,
it was usually only to be mean to him. To make matters
worse, when Joseph saw his brothers ignoring their duties
when they were supposed to be tending the sheep, he let

his father know that the flocks were not being properly watched. While Jacob was glad to know Joseph wanted to see everything go well in the fields, Joseph's brothers only hated him all the more because of his meddling. Even though Jacob loved all his sons, the others were jealous of Joseph and treated him badly.

One day, when Joseph was around seventeen years old, he had a strange dream. He told his brothers, "Listen to this dream I had: We were binding sheaves of grain out in the field when suddenly my sheaf rose and stood upright, while your sheaves gathered around mine and bowed down to it."

At this his brothers became even angrier with him. They said, "What! Do you intend to reign over us? Do you really think you will ever rule over us?" Joseph had gone too far this time. It was bad enough he had told their father when they had not been watching the sheep out in the field—what a dull, thankless job it was. But now, to have such a dream and then brag to them about it—that was even worse! "We'll take care of him first chance we get!"

But Joseph kept on dreaming his strange dreams. And, unfortunately, he kept telling his family about them, even though no one really wanted to hear about them anymore. Not long after the first dream, he told his brothers, "Listen, I had another dream, and this time the sun and moon and eleven stars were bowing down to me." This seemed ridiculous to his brothers who by now were sick of hearing about Joseph's dreams.

But when he told his father, even Jacob got angry at the idea. "What is this dream you had? Will your mother and I and your brothers actually come and bow down to the ground before you?" Such dreams and ideas were very insulting in those days. Age was a sign of high honor—people didn't bow down to seventeen-year-old shepherd boys, especially not their fathers and older brothers!

With ten older brothers, Joseph and his younger brother, Benjamin, didn't have very much work to do. Their father was a rich man, and so they did not have to work to help make ends meet. They had many fun things to do, like playing games in the tall grass at the back of their tent, or swimming in the brook. But often, the two youngest brothers were bored and looking for something to do. Joseph was glad when Jacob said to him one day, "As you know, your brothers are grazing the sheep near Shechem. I want you to go see them."

"All right, Father," Joseph replied.

So Jacob said, "Go and see if all is well with your brothers and with the flocks and bring word back to me." So Joseph left his home in the Hebron Valley and headed for Shechem.

As Joseph prepared to leave, Benjamin had begged, "Please, Joseph, take me with you."

But Joseph had replied, "You know that Father doesn't like for both of us to be away from him at the same time. You are young yet; perhaps you may go next time."

But when Joseph got to Shechem, his brothers and the flocks were not there! After he had wandered the fields looking for them with no luck, a man saw him and asked him, "What are you looking for?"

Joseph answered, "I'm looking for my brothers. Can you tell me where they are grazing their flocks?"

The man knew Joseph's brothers and had spoken with them often. "They have moved on from here. I heard them say, 'Let's go to Dothan.' "

Joseph thanked the man and set out for Dothan. But his older brothers saw him and recognized him while he was still a long way off.

"Here comes that dreamer!" they sneered to each other. "Come on, let's kill him and throw him into one of these cisterns and say that a ferocious animal devoured him. Then we'll see what comes of his dreams!"

Most of the brothers were in total agreement—they were sick to death of Joseph's being Jacob's favorite and getting all the attention with his strange dreams. Jealousy burned hot within their hearts. They were sure that no one would ever find a dead body in one of the dozens of cisterns out in the open wilderness where they were grazing their flocks. They would be able to kill Joseph without anyone ever finding out they had done it.

But Reuben, the oldest, had pity in his heart for Joseph and tried to save the boy from his jealous brothers' schemes. He knew he could not win a fight against all the others, so he decided to act as if he were in agreement with them.

"Let's not take his life," he said. "Our Law forbids the shedding of blood. Just throw him into this cistern here in the wilderness, and don't lay a hand on him. This way he'll die, but we won't shed his blood."

Reuben planned to sneak away from the camp in the middle of the night, pull his brother out, and send him back home to Jacob. He was sure that Joseph would keep silent about the whole thing since Reuben had saved his life— and maybe Joseph might keep his dreams to himself from then on.

Now Joseph was wearing a beautifully decorated robe that his father had made especially for him. It was a very special robe and had caused much jealousy among his brothers when it was given to Joseph. When he came up to where his brothers were standing, four of them grabbed him and held him down while the others stripped the robe from him.

Joseph cried out, "What are you doing, my brothers?"

They answered, "We've heard enough of your stupid dreams! Let's see what kind of dream you dream in the bottom of this cistern!"

When Joseph saw that his brothers were not simply playing a trick on him but meant to leave him to die in the cistern, he cried out for help. But there was no one to hear him in that remote place. They threw him into a cistern that had no water in it, only the limestone walls and bottom.

By this time it was evening, and the brothers sat down to

their meal. Reuben, as the oldest, took charge of posting the guards over the sheep for the night and seeing that all was in order in the camp. While he was doing this, the other brothers saw a caravan of Midianites approaching on their way to Egypt. They were carrying precious spices to trade in Egypt for gold and silver.

Judah said to the other brothers, "You know, Joseph is our brother after all, our own flesh and blood; what good would it be to us if we kill him? Instead, let's sell him to the Midianites as a slave. That way we can get rid of him without being guilty of murdering our own brother." The other brothers thought about this and agreed it was better.

As the caravan of Midianite merchants drew near, Judah called out to them, "Hello, travelers! What news from the north?"

The Midianites spoke pleasantly to Joseph's brothers in return, and soon they had a friendly conversation going. Judah then casually mentioned, "Oh, by the way, you wouldn't be interested in purchasing a slave for the Egyptian market, would you?"

The Midianite in charge of the caravan replied, "Why yes, we can always sell a slave for a good profit in Egypt."

The brothers promptly hauled Joseph up out of the cistern and handed him over, bound and gagged, to the Midianites for twenty silver coins. But Joseph's brothers kept the beautiful robe that their father, Jacob, had given him. They had a plan in mind for it.

When Reuben returned from making the rounds of the camp, he went to look in on Joseph in the cistern. In the fading light he could not be sure, but he didn't think he saw Joseph. He decided to wait until later in the night to pull Joseph out and send him home.

Later, however, he crept to the cistern in the early hours of the morning to set Joseph free. He called, softly at first and then much louder, "Joseph—Joseph, it is I, Reuben. I will pull you out and set you free!" But when he heard no answer, he went and asked his brothers, "Where is the boy Joseph?"

They replied, "While you were out, we sold him to a Midianite caravan bound for Egypt. He will not trouble us anymore!" When Reuben heard this, he tore his clothes in grief for the boy and for his father, who he knew loved Joseph greatly.

CHAPTER 2

The brothers agreed that they could not tell their father the truth about what they had done—even Reuben agreed that their wicked act had to be covered up. So they took Joseph's robe and dipped it in the blood of a goat they had killed. When they returned home several days later, they went sadly to their father and asked, "Has Joseph been sent out from the house while we were tending the flocks in the wilderness?"

Jacob, who had been growing more worried with each passing day, said anxiously, "Why, yes, I sent him out to see how it went with you. Didn't you see him?"

"No," they lied, "but we found this two days ago. Look and see whether it is your son Joseph's."

When Jacob saw that it was indeed the very robe he had given Joseph, he said, "It is my son's robe! Some ferocious animal has devoured him. Joseph has surely been torn to pieces."

Jacob went into mourning for his lost son Joseph. As was the custom of his people, he tore his clothes, put on sackcloth, and mourned for many days. All his sons and his daughters came to comfort him, but his sense of loss over his favorite son was very great. He could not be comforted. In the depths of his sorrow, he wept for many days over his son.

When Jacob's family tried to comfort him, he replied,

"No, in mourning will I go down to the grave to my son." His other sons began to deeply regret the evil they had done.

Meanwhile Joseph, very much alive, was being carried farther and farther away from the home he had always known. He was a brave lad, but at seventeen he was little more than a boy and was very frightened. He had heard about the slave trade in Egypt. Many slaves died or were treated poorly by their masters. Most worked too long in the hot sun for a few short years until their strength left them and their health failed, and then they were abandoned or put to death. He was almost overcome with fear as he thought of dying in a strange land, never seeing his father or Benjamin again. In the depths of fear and despair, Joseph's faith in the God of his fathers began to deepen.

Joseph remembered the stories his father had told of how he, Jacob, had personally wrestled with God all night long on a riverbank until God had given him a blessing. Jacob had told him of the promises the Lord had made to Jacob's grandfather Abraham and to Jacob's father, Isaac, as well as to Jacob himself. Joseph remembered how Jacob had always assured him that God would never fail him nor leave him to face trouble alone. And Joseph began to pray.

"Lord," he said, "I don't know what will happen to me. I'm alone; I'm scared, and I don't know what tomorrow will bring. I miss my father and my home and my warm bed. I don't understand why You have let this happen, Lord, but I trust You to protect me. I place my life in Your hands."

Somewhat reassured, Joseph finally managed to drop off to sleep.

The journey to Egypt took several weeks through rugged wilderness and desert. The Midianites laughed when Joseph told them it was his brothers who had sold him into slavery.

"If that's so, Boy, it doesn't change anything! You'll fetch a good price in the market. We must get our investment back on you!"

Joseph was sold to an Egyptian named Potiphar, who was the captain of the guard for Pharaoh, the king of Egypt. The Lord was with Joseph in everything he did, and, as a result, Potiphar prospered, as well. Potiphar, a shrewd man, saw that the Lord's hand was on Joseph for good. So he said, "Joseph, I will set you over all my affairs. I know your God will bless all that you do." So the Lord blessed all of Potiphar's affairs because of Joseph.

The years passed, and Joseph grew to be a handsome young man. Potiphar's wife began to notice him. She flirted with Joseph and tried to get him to neglect his work in order to spend more time with her. But Joseph said, "How can I flirt with you and spend time with you when I should be working? It would be very ungrateful toward your husband for me to do such a thing."

At this rejection, Potiphar's wife became angry and cried out, "Help! Help! This Hebrew slave has sneaked into the house to do me harm! Help! Help!" She was lying in order to get even with Joseph for rejecting her.

When Potiphar heard the story from his wife, he said to Joseph, "So this is how you repay me for setting you over all my affairs! I will do to you as you have done to me." Turning to his guards, he said, "Throw him in prison!"

Potiphar had chosen to believe his wife instead of a Hebrew slave like Joseph. So Joseph found himself once again mistreated at the hands of others.

In the prison, Joseph prayed every day to the Lord. "My God, I don't understand how this could have happened. I was a source of blessing, by Your grace, for all Potiphar's family. And it was for *refusing* to do wrong toward Potiphar that I have ended up in prison. I don't understand why You have let this happen to me. Should I have done evil so I could have stayed out of prison?"

But the Lord encouraged Joseph and blessed him even in prison. The Lord gave him favor with the warden so that he set Joseph over all the affairs of the prison, just as Potiphar had done in his house. All that Joseph did in prison went well.

Several years dragged by. The laws of Egypt did not bother too much about protecting slaves, and it looked to Joseph as if he would spend the rest of his life in prison. The days dragged into weeks, the weeks into months, and the months into years. And yet Joseph, this man so much like you and me, did one simple thing. He put his trust in God. He remembered the stories his father, Jacob, told about seeing God face-to-face; he remembered how God had made promises to Abraham, Isaac, and Jacob; he remembered the mighty things those men had seen God do for them in the face of trouble; and although he often worried, he never gave up hope. He trusted that the Lord over all the earth would do the right thing, and he prayed often to his God. And then one day something strange happened.

It seems that both the king's cupbearer and his baker had somehow offended him. Egypt's king, who was called the pharaoh, was quite angry with each of them and said to the captain of the guard, "Throw them in the guardhouse!"

The cupbearer was head over all the people who served food and drink in the king's household, and the baker was the chief baker for Pharaoh. They had failed at their duties and greatly angered Pharaoh, and he had them thrown into prison while he decided what he would do to them. In those days, kings did pretty much as they wished—there was no system of law like many modern countries have. So the chief baker and the chief cupbearer were very afraid as they were put into prison. The captain of the guard put them under Joseph's care.

After they had been in the prison for some time, the two men had dreams. The chief cupbearer had a certain dream, and it greatly troubled him as he tried to figure out what it might mean. On the same night, the chief baker had a dream, and he, too, was quite worried over what his dream might mean.

As the two men were pondering their dreams and wondering whether they had any special meaning, Joseph came in to bring them breakfast. When he saw the two men he asked them, "Why are your faces so sad today?"

They replied, "We both had dreams, but there is no one to interpret them."

"Do not interpretations belong to God?" Joseph said. "Tell me your dreams and, by the grace of God, perhaps I will be able to give you the interpretation of them."

"I will go first," said Pharaoh's chief cupbearer. "In my dream I saw a vine in front of me, and on the vine were three branches. As soon as it budded, it blossomed, and its clusters ripened into grapes. Pharaoh's cup was in my hand, and I took the grapes, squeezed them into Pharaoh's cup, and put the cup into his hand."

"What do you think it can mean?" asked the baker, now even more worried about his own dream.

"The Lord will give me the proper meaning if He so wills," replied Joseph. "I will pray and seek the Lord about this matter, and I will tell you as soon as I know what the interpretation is. Perhaps these dreams have meant nothing in particular. But we will certainly see."

Later that day, Joseph returned to the two men. "Well," the cupbearer asked anxiously, "what does it mean?"

"This is what it means," Joseph replied. "The three branches are three days. Within three days, Pharaoh will lift you up and restore you to your former position, and you will put Pharaoh's cup in his hand, just as you used to do when you were his cupbearer. But when all goes well with you, remember me and show me kindness: Mention me to Pharaoh and get me out of this prison. For I was forcibly carried off from the land of the Hebrews, and even here I have done nothing to deserve being put in a prison."

The two men were amazed that Joseph had been able to interpret the dream, and the chief cupbearer thanked him many times.

When the chief baker saw that the cupbearer's dream had been a good sign, he took heart and asked Joseph about his dream. "I, too, had a dream: On my head were three baskets of bread. In the top basket were all kinds of baked goods for Pharaoh, but the birds were eating them out of the basket on my head."

After praying about the dream, Joseph went to the baker and said, "This is what your dream means: The three baskets are three days. Within three days, Pharaoh will take off your head and hang you on a tree. And the birds will eat away your flesh."

When he heard this, the chief baker was terrified. He begged Joseph to give another interpretation, but Joseph said, "I am sorry. I can only say what the Lord has given me to say."

Three days later was Pharaoh's birthday, and he decided to throw a huge party for all of his servants and the members of his court. At a great ceremony, in the presence of all his most important officials, Pharaoh did indeed bring his chief cupbearer and his chief baker out of prison. Pharaoh restored the chief cupbearer to his former position, so that he again put the cup into the hand of Pharaoh, just as Joseph had prophesied. But the chief baker he hanged, just as the dream had foretold.

So Joseph's interpretations of both dreams came true. And although the chief cupbearer had been very grateful to Joseph when he heard the favorable interpretation of his dream, in the excitement of being restored to his former position he forgot his promise to mention Joseph to Pharaoh.

So Joseph stayed in prison. The days, weeks, and months seemed to drag on forever, and Joseph often cried out, "O mighty God, why have You let this happen to me? Have You forgotten me completely?"

Two more years passed. Then one night, Pharaoh had a dream. In the dream, Pharaoh was standing by the Nile River when seven fat, healthy cows came out of the river and began grazing on the reeds at the river's edge. After these seven came seven other cows that were thin, scrawny, and ugly. The thin, ugly cows stood beside the fat, healthy cows on the riverbank. Then the seven thin, ugly cows ate up the sleek, fat cows.

Then Pharaoh awoke from his dream in the middle of the night, and sat up in his bed. "What a strange dream!" he said to himself.

But shortly after that Pharaoh fell asleep again, and again he began to dream. This time in his dream seven full, healthy heads of grain were growing on one stalk. After these seven, seven other heads of grain sprouted—wasted, parched, and withered by the east wind. Then, just as in the other dream, the seven parched and withered heads of grain swallowed up the seven healthy, full heads of grain.

Once again Pharaoh awoke and sat up in his bed. "What a strange night this has been!" he exclaimed. "I have had not one, but two dreams that are alike and yet not alike. Surely these dreams must mean something." Pharaoh did not believe in the God of Joseph's forefathers—Pharaoh thought there were many different kinds of gods, and that one of these had sent him the dreams.

In the morning, Pharaoh said to his wise men and magicians, "I have had two strange dreams. Interpret them for me, because I am troubled by them." But when he told them the dreams, none could interpret them.

Then the chief cupbearer said to Pharaoh, "Today I am reminded of my shortcomings. Pharaoh was once angry with his servants, and he imprisoned me and the chief baker in the house of the captain of the guard. Each of us had a dream the same night, and each dream had a meaning of its own. Now a young Hebrew was there with us, a servant of the captain of the guard. We told him our dreams, and he interpreted them for us, giving each man the interpretation of his dream. And things turned out exactly as he interpreted them to us: I was restored to my position, and the other man was hanged."

When he heard this, Pharaoh commanded the captain of the guard, "Bring this man Joseph to me at once!"

The guards quickly ran and brought Joseph out of the dungeon. When he had bathed and changed his clothes, they brought him before Pharaoh.

Pharaoh said to Joseph, "I had a dream, and no one can interpret it. But I have heard it said of you that when you hear a dream you can interpret it."

"I cannot do it," Joseph replied, "but God will give

Pharaoh the answer he desires."

Then Pharaoh explained the two dreams to Joseph and said, "I told this to my magicians and wise men, but none of them could explain the meaning to me. Can your God give you the interpretation of these things?"

"Yes, O King," said Joseph, "the dreams of Pharaoh are one and the same. God has revealed to Pharaoh what He is about to do. The seven good cows are seven years, and the seven good heads of grain are seven years. The seven lean, ugly cows are seven years, and so are the seven worthless heads of grain scorched by the east wind: They are seven years of famine.

"God has shown Pharaoh that seven years of great plenty are coming through the land of Egypt, but seven years of famine will follow them. Then all the abundance in Egypt will be forgotten, because the famine that follows will be so severe. The reason the dream was given to Pharaoh in two forms is that the matter has been firmly decided, and God will do it soon."

Then Joseph said, "And now let Pharaoh look for a wise man and put him in charge of the land of Egypt. Let Pharaoh appoint commissioners over the land to take a fifth of all Egypt's harvest during the seven good years. They should collect all the food of these good years that are coming and store the grain under the authority of Pharaoh, to be kept in the cities for food. This food should be held in reserve for the country, to be used during the seven years of famine, so the country will not be ruined by the famine."

Pharaoh and his men agreed with Joseph's plan. Then Pharaoh said to his advisers, "Can we find anyone like this man, one in whom is the Spirit of God?" And they agreed that no one could be found like Joseph.

So right then and there, Pharaoh said to Joseph, "Since God has made all this known to you, there is no one as wise as you. You will be in charge of my palace, and all my people must obey your orders. Only the fact that I am the king will give me more power than I am now giving to you."

Pharaoh then took off his special ring and said to Joseph, "I hereby put you in charge of the whole land of Egypt." He put the ring on Joseph's finger, dressed him in fine linen robes, and put a gold chain around his neck. Pharaoh had Joseph ride in a chariot as his second-in-command, and people shouted, "Make way!" when he rode through.

Pharaoh said to Joseph, "I am still Pharaoh, but in everything else, no one will lift a hand or foot in all Egypt without your approval." Pharaoh renamed him Zaphenath-Paneah and gave him the beautiful Asenath to be his wife.

Now Joseph was thirty years old when all these things happened, and he went out and began to travel around Egypt as the second-in-command to Pharaoh.

During the seven good years that God had foretold in Pharaoh's dream, the land produced huge amounts of every crop. Joseph supervised a massive storage effort for the entire land of Egypt. Special cities were built just to store all the grain that was being produced.

"My lord," said Joseph's chief servant, "we have stored up so much grain in the city of Thebes that it is piled up like sand on the seashore—we cannot even begin to count it, as you have ordered us to do."

"Very well then," said Joseph, "we will no longer even try to keep a count. We can be sure that God is blessing us and that He will carry us through the seven years of famine that will eventually come."

During the good years, Joseph's wife, Asenath, gave birth to two healthy, happy sons. The first Joseph named "Manasseh," which sounds like the Hebrew word for "forget." For Joseph said, "Now God has made me forget all my trouble and all my father's household." The second son Joseph named "Ephraim," which sounds like "twice fruitful." He said, "It is because God has made me fruitful in the land where I once suffered."

But after seven years of plenty, the famine hit Egypt and all the nearby countries, just as God foretold through Joseph. The nearby countries began to feel the famine, because they had not been warned as Egypt had. But in Egypt there was food. As the famine got worse, the Egyptian people came to Pharaoh for help, and he said, "Do as Joseph tells you."

Soon the famine had spread throughout the entire country of Egypt, and it became time for Joseph to use the wisdom and guidance that the Lord had given him for just such troubled times. Joseph had all the great storehouses in each city opened up, and the grain that had been brought in from the surrounding fields and stored in each city was ready to be sold to all the people. Pharaoh had taken one-fifth of all the crops produced in the land during the good years as a tax on the farmers. Now Pharaoh had grain and other produce to sell to the Egyptian people to keep them alive. Not only that, but all the neighboring countries came to Egypt to buy grain and other supplies, because the famine was very bad all over the world. Only Egypt had been prepared, thanks to Joseph's God.

Jacob, Joseph's father, soon learned back in Canaan that Egypt still had grain that it was willing to sell to other people. He said to his remaining sons, "Why are you sitting around looking at each other? I hear that there is grain for sale in Egypt. Go down there and buy some for us so that we will not have to die."

Jacob sent the ten older brothers to Egypt to buy grain. But he did not send Benjamin, the youngest, because Benjamin had become his favorite after Joseph had disappeared, and he was afraid that something bad might happen to Benjamin also. So Jacob's sons went down to Egypt, along with other people of every description, because only Egypt still had grain to sell.

It so happened that Joseph, as the governor of the land under Pharaoh, was the one in charge of selling grain both to the Egyptians and to those from other countries. Imagine his surprise when one day ten dusty, bearded Hebrews stumbled in, tired from their long journey, and bowed down to him with their faces to the ground!

"O great Zaphenath-Paneah, governor of all Egypt," they said, "please allow your humble servants to buy some grain for our starving families." They did not recognize him because it had been many years since they last saw him, and he had grown to manhood—but Joseph recognized his brothers.

"Where do you come from?" he asked them through an interpreter, speaking sternly and pretending to be a stranger.

They replied, "We have come from the land of Canaan to buy food." It was then that Joseph remembered his dreams about his brothers' bowing down to him. The dreams had come to pass, but he felt no joy about it. He decided to test his brothers to see what kind of men they had become.

"You are spies!" he cried. "You have come to see where our land is unprotected!"

"No, my lord, we only want food. We are honest men, all sons of one man. Our youngest brother is with our father in Canaan, and one brother is no more."

"Well then, here is how I will test you. One of you may go back and bring this youngest brother. The rest will be kept in prison till he returns. If you are lying, I will know you are spies!" And he threw them in prison.

Joseph let his brothers stew in prison for three days. On the third day, he had them brought before him and spoke to them again.

"Do this, and you will live," he told them, "for I fear God and will act fairly. If you are honest men, let one of your brothers stay here in prison while the rest of you go and take grain back for your starving households. But you must bring your youngest brother to me so that your words may be proved true and that you may not die."

Then Joseph's brothers began to talk among themselves, believing that as an Egyptian he could not understand their speech—he had been speaking to them through an interpreter. They said, "Surely we are being punished by the Lord because of what we did to Joseph."

"We saw how distressed Joseph was when he pleaded with us for his life, but we wouldn't listen. That's why this distress has come upon us."

"Didn't I tell you not to sin against the boy?" asked Reuben. "But you wouldn't listen. Now we must give an accounting for the blood we spilled."

Joseph had to turn his back to his brothers, he was so overcome with emotion at hearing that they had repented and were sorry that they had done such an evil thing to him so many years before. He wept silently with a mixture of grief and joy—grief that he had ever had to be taken away from his family by the cruel thing his brothers had done, and joy that they had become men of character who were able to learn from their mistakes and to repent of them before the Lord.

But then Joseph stopped weeping, dried his eyes, and

turned to face his brothers once again. He was not through testing them—not yet. He had his brother Simeon taken from them by his guards, and right in front of them had him placed in chains.

"In this way will your words be tested to see if you are telling the truth," he said to them. "If you are not, then as surely as Pharaoh lives, you are spies! I will keep this one while you return to Canaan and feed your starving families. But then you must return to Egypt, and you had better bring this youngest brother back with you."

His brothers again began to protest their innocence, saying, "My lord, it is just as we have told you—"

But Joseph cut them off and would not hear any more.

"Go back to your rooms now and prepare to return to Canaan. Your brother will be kept safely here until you return. You need not fear for him, if you are telling the truth. But if you are lying, then you will not see my face in order to speak with me again."

Joseph spoke to the men who attended him, "Fill each man's bags with grain, as much as they will hold, and give each man of the provisions he will need for the journey back to Canaan." And then, calling the chief steward aside, he spoke to him quietly. "I want you to place each man's silver, that he has given in payment, back in his sack of grain."

All these commands were carried out by Joseph's men. As soon as all the preparations were completed, Joseph's brothers left for Canaan.

After a long day's journey, Joseph's nine remaining brothers stopped to rest for the night. As one of the brothers opened one of the sacks to get some grain out to feed his donkey, he saw a small bag in the mouth of the sack.

"What could this be?" he wondered out loud, and pulled the sack from the larger sack of grain. He opened the drawstring, and out into his open hand tumbled several silver coins from the land of Canaan!

Astonished, he ran back to the campfire with the silver and said in a quavering voice, "My silver has been returned. Here it is in my sack!"

The men did not know what to make of this and turned to each other in great confusion and fear. Their hearts sank as they wondered, "What is this that God has done to us?" Yet no one thought then to search his bags further.

When the nine brothers returned to their father, Jacob, they told him all about their trip and the strange things that had happened. They said, "The man who is lord over the land spoke harshly to us and treated us as though we were spying on their land. We denied it and explained to him that we are all brothers, and that we are honest men.

"Then the man who is lord over the land said to us, 'This is how I will know whether you are honest men: Leave one of your brothers here with me and take food for your starving households and go. But bring your youngest brother to me so I will know that you are not spies but honest men. Then I will give your brother back to you, and you can trade in the land.' "

Then, as they began to unpack from the journey, each man found in his sack his pouch of silver that had been given in payment for the grain in Egypt! They all became frightened, and Jacob said, "You have deprived me of my children. Joseph is no more, and Simeon is no more, and now you want to take Benjamin. Everything is against me!"

Then Reuben, the eldest, replied, "You may put both of *my* sons to death if I do not bring Benjamin back to you. Entrust him to my care, and I will bring him back."

But Jacob said, "My son will not go down to Egypt with you. Now that Joseph is dead, he is the only one I have left. If harm comes to him on the journey you are taking, it will bring my gray head down to the grave in sorrow."

The family of Jacob could not agree on what to do next, so they did nothing. But the famine continued throughout the land so that finally Jacob instructed his sons, "Go back and see if you can't buy just a little more grain in Egypt."

But Judah said to him, "The man there warned us sternly, 'You will not see me to talk to me again unless your brother is with you.' If you send Benjamin along with us, we will go down and buy food for all the families. But if you won't let Benjamin come with us, there is no point in going, because the man will not speak to us unless we bring our youngest brother."

At this the old man Jacob wrung his hands and cried out in sorrow. "Why must my sons be taken from me?"

Jacob wept aloud in distress over the problem he had to face. Then he turned to his sons and shouted, "Why did you bring this trouble on me by telling the man you had another brother?"

"It is not really our fault, Father," replied Asher soothingly. "This Egyptian questioned us in great detail about ourselves and our family. He asked, 'Is your father still living? Do you have another brother?' All we did was answer his questions; we could hardly have done otherwise. He would not have sold us the grain if we had been unwilling to answer his questions. We simply answered the questions he put to us. How were we to know he would say to us, 'Bring your brother down here'?" And all Asher's brothers said the same thing to their father.

Then Judah spoke up. He said, "Send the boy Benjamin along with me, and we will go at once, so that we and you and our many children may continue to live and not die in this famine. I will guarantee his safety: You can hold me personally responsible for him. If I do not bring him back to you safe and sound and set him down right here in front of you, I will bear the blame before you all the rest of my life. But as it is right now with all this talk, we could have been there and back again twice by now if we hadn't delayed."

All the brothers began to talk at once so that no one could make himself understood above the others. Finally, Jacob raised his hand to silence them. "I have made my decision," he announced.

"You, Reuben, and you, Judah, know more than anyone else what Joseph and now Benjamin have meant to me. And you two have been willing to put up your own sons and your honor for Benjamin so that you may buy back Simeon and bring back grain so that we will not starve. It pleases me to know that you have begun to follow the God of your forefathers and to do what is good and right, no matter what the cost. I will tell you now that I have often wondered whether you would be God-fearing men or not, and I have not always believed everything you told me."

The two brothers hung their heads in shame at this, since they knew he was speaking about what they had told him about Joseph.

Then Jacob paused and drew a long breath. "So, if it must be, I will entrust Benjamin to you, though I fear I will yet lose him. Take the best products of our land down to the man as a gift—a little honey, balm, some spices and myrrh, pistachio nuts, and almonds. And take double the silver back with you, since you will have to return the silver we found in the mouths of your sacks. Perhaps it was a mistake. Take your brother Benjamin, also, and go back to the man at once. And may God Almighty grant you mercy before the man so that he will let Simeon and Benjamin come back with you." Then the old man began to weep again under the great pain of seeing his youngest being carried away to face this powerful stranger. "But as for me," he said, "I am bereaved, I am bereaved."

Chapter 4

Although the brothers tried to console their father, they could not. So they took the gifts, all the silver, and their youngest brother, Benjamin, and hurried back down to Egypt to present themselves before Joseph.

When Joseph saw that Benjamin was with them, he told his steward, "Take these men to my house and prepare the noon meal for me to eat with them."

But Joseph's brothers did not understand the command he gave, since he spoke in Egyptian. So when they came to his house, they thought to themselves, "He is bringing us here because of the silver that was put into our sacks the first time. He wants to attack us and overpower us, take our donkeys, and make us his slaves so that he can recover the money he lost when we somehow had the silver put back into our bags!"

So immediately the brothers spoke up to the steward, saying, "Please, Sir, we came down here the first time to buy food. But at the first place we camped for the night, one of us opened his sack and found his silver, the exact amount, in the mouth of his sack. Then, when we had all returned home, we found that there was silver in everyone's sack. So we have brought it back with us. We have also brought additional silver with us to buy more food. We don't know who put our silver in our sacks."

The steward, who had returned their silver at Joseph's orders, knew Joseph did not mean to harm them. He reassured them. "It's all right," he said, "don't be afraid. Your God, the God of your father, has given you treasure in your sacks; I myself received the silver you had last time. And now," he continued, "I have a surprise for you."

The steward snapped his fingers at a servant waiting nearby, who disappeared into the interior of the house. Within a few moments he returned, leading Simeon into the front room!

"My brothers, my beloved brothers!" he beamed. "I knew you would return for me."

"How have you been? How were you treated?" they all asked at once, still nervous about how they would be received by this stern Egyptian and still wondering about the silver in their sacks.

"Oh, fine, fine!" he said cheerfully. "Zaphenath-Paneah is a busy man, yet he has come to speak with me through an interpreter once a week since you left. He asks me everything about our families, our wives, and children. I have really been under house arrest here—I've not been in the prison."

The brothers were surprised to hear that Simeon had not been kept in prison, and they were frightened to hear that the stern Egyptian governor had been finding out even more about their families. What would he demand of them next?

The steward then took the brothers into Joseph's house

and gave them water to wash their feet and gave them food for their donkeys. He told them they would be eating with Joseph at noon, so they made their gifts ready to present to him when he arrived.

When Joseph came home, they presented to him the gifts they had brought, and again his brothers all bowed low before him, their faces touching the ground. He began by asking them how they were.

"We have been fine, my lord, except that the famine continues," they replied.

"How is your aged father you told me about? Is he still living?" They did not notice how the man anxiously leaned forward as he asked this question.

"Your servant our father is still alive and well." And again they bowed before him to show him honor.

As his eyes lit upon Benjamin, his beloved brother, he asked, "Is this your youngest brother, the one you told me about?" And he said, "God be gracious to you, my son." Joseph became greatly moved as he looked upon the face of his most beloved younger brother whom he had not seen for so long. He had to quickly excuse himself from their presence and hurry outside to find a place to weep in secret.

After Joseph had managed to bring himself under control, he washed his face and returned to the dining hall. "Serve the food," he said.

According to the practices of the Egyptians, Joseph was served by himself, the Egyptians at the meal were served by themselves, and Joseph's brothers were served at yet another table, because Egyptians did not like to eat at the same table as Hebrews. His brothers were astonished to see that they had been seated at the table in the order of their ages. "How did he know who was oldest and who came next in order?" they asked one another. When they were finally served their food, Benjamin received five times as much as anyone else at their table. All Joseph's brothers had a good time at the feast and laughed and talked freely.

"My honored guests, men of Canaan," Joseph began, when the time for speeches came. "I have tested you to see whether indeed you were honest men, as you claimed. . ." Here he paused dramatically, for effect, ". . .and I am pleased to see that you have in no way disappointed me." All Joseph's brothers breathed a sigh of relief.

"You are indeed honest men, sons of one father, and not spies, as I had originally feared. Please accept my apologies and be assured that, in the morning, you will all be free to depart and return with all haste to your families in Canaan, who I am sure are waiting for the food that you will take them."

Reuben, the oldest, arose after Joseph's speech had been fully translated and said, "Thank you, my lord. We will do as you say."

But as his brothers were packing the next morning, Joseph said to his steward, "Fill each sack completely, and again put each man's silver in the mouth of his sack. Then put my special silver cup in the mouth of the youngest one's sack." The steward did as he was told.

Shortly after his brothers set out, Joseph sent the steward after them, saying, "When you catch up to them, say, 'Why have you repaid good with evil? Isn't this the cup my master drinks from and also uses for divination? This is a wicked thing you have done.' "

So the steward and his men rode furiously after Joseph's brothers and soon caught up with them and stopped them. And when they halted the caravan, the steward confronted Reuben and repeated the words Joseph had given him to say.

When they were confronted by the steward in this manner, Joseph's brothers became very angry.

"Why does my lord say such things? Far be it from your servants to do anything like that! We even brought back to you from the land of Canaan the silver we found inside the mouths of our sacks! So why would we steal silver or gold from your master's house? If any of your servants is found to have it, he will die; and the rest of us will become your slaves."

Now this was a foolish thing for Joseph's brothers to say, even if they were angry and very sure that none of them had done such a thing. They had quickly forgotten the strange events of their first trip and the silver in their sacks!

"Rash words indeed," said the steward, "but I will hold you to them! Let it be as you say. Whoever is found to have the cup will become my slave; the rest of you will be free from blame."

Each of the brothers quickly took his sack down from his

donkey and opened it for inspection. Then the steward searched each sack in turn, beginning with Reuben and ending with Benjamin, the youngest. Of course, the cup was found in Benjamin's sack, right where the steward had put it!

The brothers, astonished, tore their clothes in grief. Silently, they each mounted their donkeys and returned to the city, determined to keep their youngest brother from becoming the slave of a foreign master.

Joseph's brothers came before him in his house and threw themselves at his feet. He said to them, "What is this you have done? Don't you know a man like me can find things out by divination?" He said this to frighten them. Joseph did not really practice divination, since it was an evil thing. Joseph got all his guidance from the Lord.

"What can we say to my lord?" said Judah. "How can we prove our innocence? God has uncovered your servants' guilt. We are now my lord's slaves—we ourselves and the one who was found to have the cup." Judah would rather have become a slave in a foreign country than have to go back and face his father after losing Benjamin.

But Joseph said, "Only the thief will be my slave; the rest may go."

Then Judah came closer and asked, "Please let me have a word with you. You asked us, my lord, about our family, and we told you about our aged father and our youngest brother, much loved by our father. Then you said to your servants, 'Bring him down to me so I can see him for myself.' And we said to you, 'The boy cannot leave his father; if he leaves him, his father will die.' But you told us, your servants, 'Unless your youngest brother comes down with you, you will not see my face again.' When we went back to our father, we told him what you had said.

"When our father sent us back to get more grain this time, we warned him, 'We cannot go down. Only if Benjamin is with us will we go. We cannot see the man's face unless our youngest brother is with us.'

"So now, if the boy is not with us when I go back to my father, and if my father, whose life is closely bound up with the boy's life, sees that the boy isn't there, he will die. We will have brought the gray head of our father down to the grave in sorrow. I, your servant, guaranteed the boy's safety to my father. I said, 'If I do not bring him back to you, I will bear the blame before you all my life!'

"Now then, please let your servant remain here as my lord's slave in place of the boy, and let the boy return with his brothers. How can I go back to my father if the boy is not with me? No! Do not let me see the misery that would come upon my father." So Judah offered to take his brother's place as a slave in a strange country, to spare his father grief.

When Joseph saw the great sacrifice that Judah, who had formerly treated him so badly, was willing to make for his father and for Benjamin, he could stand it no longer. "Have everyone leave my presence!" he cried. Joseph wept so loudly that the Egyptians heard him even outside the room, and they told Pharaoh's household about it later.

Joseph then cried out to his brothers, in their own Hebrew language, "I am Joseph!" They stared at him, stricken with shock and amazement.

"Is my father still living?" he asked, hardly daring to hope that it could be so, since Jacob had been an old man when Joseph had been carried off so many years before. But his brothers were so terrified of him that they couldn't answer.

Then Joseph said to them, "Come close to me," and they did so. Then he said, "I am indeed your brother Joseph, the one you sold into Egypt! And now, do not be distressed and do not be angry with yourselves for selling me here, because it was to save lives that God sent me ahead of you. For two years now there has been famine in the land, and for the next five years there will not be any farming. But God sent me ahead of you to preserve for you a remnant on earth and to save your lives by a great deliverance.

"So then, it was not you who sent me here, but God. He made me father to Pharaoh, lord of his entire household, and ruler of all Egypt. Now hurry back to my father and give him this message."

Then Joseph told them, "Say to Jacob, 'This is what your son Joseph says, "God has made me lord of all Egypt. Come down to me; don't delay. You shall live in the region of Goshen and be near me—you, your children and grandchildren, your flocks and herds, and all you have. I will provide for you there, because five years of famine are still to come. Otherwise you and your household and all who belong to you will become poor." '

"You can see for yourselves, and so can my brother Benjamin, that it is really I who am speaking to you. Tell my father about all the honor accorded me in Egypt and about everything you have seen. And bring my father down here quickly."

For a long moment they all continued to stare at Joseph in silence.

Then, all at once, the joy of being reunited with his family, and of being restored to them as a true brother and not an enemy, completely overwhelmed Joseph. He stepped down quickly from the platform, threw his arms around his youngest brother Benjamin and wept once again, this time for pure joy. Benjamin embraced his brother, lost for so long and now somehow found once again, and he, too, wept for joy.

Joseph kissed all his brothers, as the Hebrews did on very joyous occasions, and wept over each one of them. He reunited with them as their brother, at long last.

"I have dreamed of this moment for years!" he exclaimed.

"Brother, that is one dream of yours we are happy to hear about," said Reuben, and they all laughed together.

Then the brothers spent several hours together talking of many things. When Pharaoh heard that Joseph's brothers had come to Egypt, he was pleased and sent word to Joseph, "Tell your brothers, 'Do this: Load your animals and return to the the land of Canaan and bring your father and your families back to me. I will give you the best of the land of Egypt, and you can enjoy the fat of the land.'

"Also tell them, 'Take some carts from Egypt for your children and your wives, and get your father and come right back to the land of Egypt. Never mind about your belongings, because the best of all Egypt will be yours.' " And Joseph told his brothers all that the king of Egypt had said for them to do.

So Joseph's brothers agreed to do as Pharaoh had said. Joseph gave each of them carts and supplies for the journey, but to Benjamin he gave three hundred coins of silver and five sets of clothes. To his father, Jacob, Joseph sent ten donkeys loaded with the best products of the land of Egypt, and ten donkeys carrying the things Jacob would need for his journey down to Egypt from the land of Canaan. These donkeys carried grain, bread, and many other supplies, because it took many long days to journey on the back of a donkey from Canaan to Egypt.

Joseph sent his brothers off saying, "Don't argue on the way!" They departed on the long trip and spent many days journeying back to their father, Jacob, in Canaan.

CHAPTER 5

When the eleven brothers returned safely to Jacob in Canaan, he was greatly relieved to see them. But he could not believe it when they said, "Joseph is still alive! In fact, he is ruler of all Egypt!" But after he had seen all the things they had brought back and the twenty donkeys sent by Joseph especially for him, his heart was gladdened.

"I'm convinced!" he exclaimed. "My son Joseph is still alive. I will go and see him before I die."

Several days were needed to prepare for the journey, since Jacob and all his sons and daughters and all their spouses and children would be leaving Canaan, never to return. But before too long, everything was ready, and they set off for Egypt with Jacob leading them.

When they reached the encampment of Beersheba, Jacob offered sacrifices to God just as his father, Isaac, had done. God spoke to Jacob (whom God had renamed Israel when Jacob wrestled with God), and said, "Jacob! Jacob!"

"Hear I am," replied Jacob.

"I am God, the God of your father," He said. "Do not be afraid to go down to Egypt, for I will make you a great nation there. I will go down to Egypt with you, and I will surely bring your descendants back out of there at a later time, a great and powerful nation. And when you die, your beloved son Joseph will close your eyes with his own hand." These words were a great comfort to Jacob, because he remembered the promises God had made beforehand and knew that God would keep His promise.

The family again packed up their belongings and headed for Egypt, because Jacob was eager to see his long-lost son. The group left Beersheba, traveling in the carts that Pharaoh had given the sons when they left Egypt to get Jacob and bring him back. Jacob's family—his sons and daughters, his grandchildren and even a few great-grandchildren—all went down to Egypt with Jacob when he decided to leave Canaan. They took all the things they owned, including all their sheep, cattle, and other livestock. Jacob took down to Egypt his sons Reuben, Simeon, Levi, Judah, Issachar, Zebulun, Gad, Asher, Dan, Naphtali, and Benjamin, his daughter Dinah, and all their children. All together, sixty-six members of Jacob's family went down to Egypt.

Jacob told his son Judah to go on ahead of the main party of travelers, so that Judah could make sure that they were going in the right direction and would reach Egypt as they planned. It was difficult in those days to cross large areas of desert and wastelands and make sure that you were always headed in the right direction. So Judah went ahead just to make sure. The group had done a good job, however, and would soon arrive at the region of Goshen at the border of Egypt. When Joseph heard they would soon reach Goshen, he traveled to Goshen in his personal chariot to meet his father.

When father and son met again after so many years, Joseph ran to Jacob and gave him a big hug. For a long time, he just hugged his father and wept.

After awhile, Joseph stepped back, looked into Jacob's eyes, and smiled.

"Somehow, I always believed that I would see you again, Father! I had faith that our God would allow it to come to pass."

"I had no reason for my hope, my son, since I was told that you had been killed," said Jacob, "yet I continued to hope that somehow it wasn't true. I have prayed every day that you might somehow be restored to me. Now, after many long years, I have finally had my prayers answered. Now I am ready to die in peace, since I have seen for myself that you are still alive."

"Let us rejoice together, all of us, to be together again after all that has happened," said Levi, "and let us not fail to give thanks to our God!"

Then Joseph said to all Jacob's family that was assembled there, "I will go up and say to Pharaoh, 'My family who were living in Canaan have come to me. The men are shepherds; they tend livestock, and they have brought along their flocks and herds and everything they own.' When Pharaoh calls you in and asks, 'What is your occupation?' you should answer, 'Your servants have tended livestock from our boyhood on, just as our fathers did.' Then you will be allowed to settle in Goshen, a rich and fertile region, because Egyptians do not like shepherds. Therefore they will be happy for all of us to settle out here at the edge of their land where they will not have to come near us too often."

All the brothers and his father agreed on this plan.

So Joseph chose five of his brothers to present personally before Pharaoh and took them with him to visit the king.

Pharaoh asked them, "What is your occupation?"

"Your servants are shepherds," they replied, "just as our fathers were. We have come to live here awhile, because the famine is severe in Canaan, and your servants' flocks have no pasture. So now, please let your servants settle in Goshen."

Pharaoh then spoke to Joseph. "Your father and your brothers have come to you, and the land of Egypt is before you; settle your father and your brothers in the best part of the land. Let them live in Goshen. And if you know of any among them with special ability, put them in charge of my own livestock."

Then Pharaoh told Joseph to bring Jacob before him. The old man greeted Pharaoh according to custom, then Pharaoh asked him, "How old are you?"

Jacob spoke slowly, "The years of my life are a hundred and thirty. My years have been few and difficult, and they do not equal the years of the lives of my fathers." Pharaoh sat silently before the stooped old man who had seen so many things in his life, and who had personally wrestled with God Almighty on a lonely riverbank many years before, and he could think of nothing else to say. So Jacob said farewell to

Pharaoh and left his presence.

Joseph settled his father, his brothers, and their wives and children, and his sister and her family in the region of Goshen as Pharaoh had said.

Even though Joseph was able to provide for his family that had come down from Canaan, the rest of the people of Egypt and Canaan were having a very hard time because of the famine. Over several years, they finally spent all the money they had to buy food, and still the famine continued. So the people came to Joseph and said, "Give us food so we won't die; our money is all gone."

Joseph replied, "Then bring me your livestock in exchange for more grain."

The Egyptians did that until their livestock all belonged to Pharaoh. Then they came to Joseph and said, "The famine is still going on. All we have left is our land and ourselves; make us Pharaoh's slaves so we can have more food."

So Joseph bought all the land in Egypt for his master, Pharaoh.

The people of Egypt had no choice but to become Pharaoh's slaves, since they had nothing left to sell except their land and their services. They could not hold out against the famine any longer. So all the people of Egypt became Pharaoh's slaves except for the Egyptian priests, who did not serve the Lord but served the gods of the Egyptians. Because these priests received food from Pharaoh already, they had enough to live on and did not have to sell their land or themselves to Pharaoh.

The people of Egypt had pleaded with Joseph saying, "Give us seed so that we may live and not die, and that the land may not become desolate." Joseph had shown mercy to them and had also been faithful in doing business for his master, Pharaoh, by accepting their land and their services.

Joseph told the Egyptian people, "Now that I have bought you and your land today for Pharaoh, here is seed for you so you can plant the ground. But when the crop comes in, give a fifth of it to Pharaoh. The other four-fifths of it you may keep as seed for the fields and as food for yourselves and your households and your children."

"You have saved our lives," the Egyptians replied. "May we find favor in the eyes of our lord; we will be in bondage to Pharaoh."

From that time onward, it became a law in the land of Egypt that the king would receive a fifth of all the crops produced by all the people. Also, all the land of all the people, except for the priests', became the property of Pharaoh.

CHAPTER 6

Jacob and his sons prospered greatly in Goshen, and they lived there seventeen more years, until Jacob reached the age of one hundred forty-seven. Then Jacob became aware that he would soon die. He called for his favorite son, Joseph, and spoke to him.

"If I have found favor in your eyes, put your hand under my thigh and promise that you will show me kindness and faithfulness." The people of those times would put their hand under their father's or their master's leg much like we raise our right hands today—it showed that they meant to keep their promise and were not lying.

"Do not bury me in Egypt," Jacob said, "but when I rest with my fathers, carry me out of Egypt and bury me where they are buried."

God had promised Jacob, as He had promised Jacob's father and grandfather before him, that God would make his descendants into a mighty nation. This nation would be named "Israel," the new name for Jacob that had been given to him by God Himself.

Jacob knew that God would keep this promise. And he wanted to be buried in the land that God had said would someday belong to this great nation Israel. So he said to Joseph, "Swear to me that you will bury me in Canaan where my fathers are buried."

"I will do as you say," said Joseph.

"Swear to me," said his father.

Then Joseph swore to his father as Jacob had asked, and when Jacob saw that his son would be faithful to carry out the promise, he worshipped God as he leaned on the top of his staff.

Not too long after Joseph visited his father and swore to bury him in the Promised Land, he received word that his father was sick. When they told Jacob, "Your son Joseph has come to you," he took strength and managed to sit up on his sickbed.

Jacob told his son, "God Almighty appeared to me at Luz in the land of Canaan, and there He blessed me and said to me, 'I am going to make you fruitful and will increase your numbers. I will make you a community of peoples, and I will give this land as an everlasting possession to your descendants after you.'

"Now then, your two sons born to you in Egypt before I came to you here will be counted as mine; Ephraim and Manasseh will be mine, just as my own sons Reuben and Simeon and all the others are mine.

"Any children born to you after them will be counted as yours and will inherit territory under the names of Ephraim and Manasseh." Then Jacob saw Ephraim and Manasseh at the far end of the room and asked Joseph, "Who are these two?"

Joseph answered, "They are the sons God has given me

here in Egypt. These are Ephraim and Manasseh."

"Bring them to me so I may bless them." Blessings in those days were very important to those who received them. A blessing spoken by a man of God like Jacob was really a prophecy, a statement of what God was going to bring about in their lives.

Jacob's eyes were failing because of his great age, so that he could hardly see. So Joseph brought his sons right up to Jacob.

Jacob began by saying to Joseph, "I never expected to see your face again, and now God has allowed me to see your children, too."

Joseph then placed Manasseh, the older brother, so that Jacob could put his right hand on Manasseh's head; this was the place of greater honor and belonged to the older brother. But Jacob crossed his hands so that his right hand was on Ephraim's head, and his left hand on Manasseh's.

Jacob then blessed Joseph, saying, "May the God before whom my fathers walked, the God who has been my shepherd all my life to this day, the angel who has delivered me from all harm—may He bless these boys. May they be called by my name and by the names of my fathers Abraham and Isaac, and may they increase greatly upon the earth."

At that point, Joseph noticed that his father had crossed his hands. He took his father's hands to uncross them and said, "No, my father, this one is the firstborn; put your right hand on his head."

But Jacob said, "I know, my son, I know. He, too, will become a people when his descendants increase, and his name will become famous. But his younger brother will be even greater than he; his descendants will become a group of nations."

Then Jacob blessed them. "In your name will Israel pronounce this blessing: 'May God make you like Ephraim and Manasseh.'"

Then Jacob said to Joseph, "I am about to die, but God will be with you and take you back to the land of your fathers. And since you are over your brothers, I give you one portion more of the land than I am giving to your brothers."

Jacob then said, "Gather my sons around me so that I can tell them what will happen to them in the days and years to come." Jacob was a mighty man of God who would speak the words God gave him to say, so his sons would know what would happen to them in the future. Jacob told them how the people would live who would grow up from their sons and grandsons and their later descendants into a mighty nation that would have the name Israel, that would inherit the Promised Land of Canaan and make it their own.

Many of the things Jacob said were not clear to his sons, because prophets often use words in a way that could mean more than one thing. At other times they talk about animals or strange things just to show their listeners a different way of seeing things.

"Assemble and listen, sons of Jacob," he began. "Listen to

your father Israel." He then spoke to each of his sons in turn, telling them about what they had done to deserve the things that would happen to their descendants. Most of the things he described would not take place while his sons were still alive but only after they had died.

Since Reuben, the oldest son, had done many evil things to his father over the years, he lost his rights as the firstborn son. Jacob said to him, "Reuben, you are my firstborn, my might, the first sign of my strength, excelling in honor, excelling in power. Turbulent as the waters, you will no longer excel, for you sinned against me when you were younger, and you will not be forgiven for it."

Jacob then called the next two in order of their birth, Simeon and Levi. Many years before, these two had taken revenge on some men who had done something wrong to their sister Dinah. But since the Lord is the one who should take revenge, Jacob had this to say to Simeon and Levi:

"Simeon and Levi are brothers—their swords are weapons of violence. Let me not enter their council, let me not join their assembly, for they have killed men in their anger and hamstrung oxen as they pleased. Cursed be their anger, so fierce, and their fury, so cruel! I will scatter them in the land of Jacob and disperse them in Israel."

Jacob spoke to them for the Lord, telling them what would happen to the tribes that would bear their names that would come in later generations.

Next, Jacob called his son Judah in front of him. Judah

had often been a leader of the brothers. Jacob had many good things to say to him:

"Judah, your brothers will praise you; your hand will be on the neck of your enemies; your father's sons will bow down to you. You are a lion's cub, O Judah; you return from the prey, my son. The scepter will not depart from Judah, nor the ruler's staff from between his feet, until the one comes to whom it belongs and all the nations give him their obedience. He will tether his donkey to a vine, his colt to the choicest branch; he will wash his garments in wine, his robes in the blood of grapes. His eyes will be darker than wine, his teeth whiter than milk."

Jacob then spoke to Zebulun, Issachar, and Dan.

"Zebulun will live by the seashore and become a haven for ships; his border will extend toward Sidon.

"Issachar is a rawboned donkey lying down between two saddlebags. When he sees how good his resting place is, and how pleasant his land, he will bend his shoulder to the burden and submit to forced labor.

"Dan will provide justice for his people as one of the tribes of Israel. Dan will be a serpent by the roadside, a viper along the path, that bites the horse's heels so that its rider tumbles backward. I look for your deliverance, O Lord," Jacob ended.

"Now come forth, Gad, Asher, and Naphtali, and hear the blessings I speak to you from the Lord.

"Gad will be attacked by a band of raiders, but he will

attack them at their heels.

"Asher's food will be rich; he will provide delicacies fit for a king.

"Naphtali is a doe set free that bears beautiful fawns."

It was difficult for the brothers to understand just what the Lord was saying to them through these words, but the things Jacob had said were pleasant and seemed to mean that their tribes would do well in the Promised Land. The three brothers were pleased at what their father had told them.

"Now let Joseph, my beloved son, come forth."

Joseph stepped forward to receive his blessing, bringing Ephraim and Manasseh before Jacob since he had said they would be treated as Jacob's own sons. "Speak your blessings to these my sons," said Joseph, "so that they may hear it."

Jacob then spoke to Joseph and his sons.

"Joseph is a fruitful vine, a fruitful vine near a spring, whose branches climb over a wall. With bitterness archers attacked him; they shot at him with hostility. But his bow remained steady, his strong arms stayed limber, because of the hand of the Mighty One of Jacob, because of the Shepherd, the Rock of Israel, because of our father's God, Who helps you, because of the Almighty, Who blesses you with blessings of the heavens above, blessings of the deep that lies below, blessings of the breast and womb. Your father's blessings are greater than the blessings of the ancient mountains, than the bounty of the age-old hills. Let all these rest on the head of Joseph, on the brow of the prince among his brothers."

Joseph was deeply moved at hearing the rich blessings God would provide to his children, especially after the years he had suffered in Egypt as a prisoner and a slave. "Thank you, Father," was all he could say.

"It is a good blessing!" all his brothers cried. "Praise the Lord for his faithfulness to Joseph!" They were glad that Joseph had received great blessing from God.

"Well, Father," said Benjamin, "as the youngest, I always seem to be going last. I hope you have saved a blessing for me."

"Yes, of course, my son. Listen: Benjamin is a ravenous wolf; in the morning he devours the prey, in the evening he divides the plunder."

His brothers laughed and cheered at this prophecy; they could not picture their little brother as a ravenous wolf, no matter how hard they tried.

CHAPTER 7

And so Jacob told his sons what would come to pass to the tribes of people that would grow up from all their descendants. One day, several hundred years later, they would be called by God to go up out of Egypt and take over the land that God had promised to Jacob's forefathers and to Jacob and his descendants. It would not happen during Jacob's lifetime, nor Joseph's, nor the lifetimes of Joseph's children or grandchildren. But in God's timing, according to God's plan, He would one day raise up a leader who would take the twelve tribes, descended from these twelve sons of Israel, and lead them into the Promised Land of Canaan. And then all these prophecies that Jacob had spoken would come to pass, because Jacob had spoken for the Lord.

Then Jacob spoke again to his sons. "I am about to be gathered to my people." By this Jacob meant he was about to die. "Bury me with my fathers in the cave in the field of Machpelah, near Mamre in Canaan, which my grandfather Abraham bought from the Hittites. That is the place where my grandfather Abraham and my grandmother Sarah are buried, and where my father, Isaac, and my mother, Rebekah, are buried, and that is where I buried my wife Leah. So please make sure you do as my son Joseph has promised me and carry my body back to Canaan to be buried with all the rest of my people."

As soon as he had finished saying these things to his sons, Jacob lay back down on the bed, took a deep breath, and died.

When Jacob's sons saw that he was dead, they tore their clothes as the Hebrews do when they are very sad, and they began to weep for their dead father. All Jacob's twelve sons, his daughter Dinah, and all their wives and children and grandchildren began to weep and mourn for the great man who had just died. Jacob was a beloved father and grandfather and the leader of their clan. Joseph flung himself down upon his father's body and began to weep in sorrow.

After some time, Joseph called for the doctors of Egypt who served him to come and prepare Jacob to be buried. These doctors spent forty days applying special lotions and herbs to the body, preparing it for burial. The Egyptians mourned seventy days for Jacob according to their customs.

Once the time of mourning had passed, Joseph spoke to those in Pharaoh's court. "If I have found favor in your eyes," he said, "speak to Pharaoh for me. Tell him, 'My father made me swear an oath and said, "I am about to die; bury me in the tomb I dug for myself in the land of Canaan." Now let me go up and bury my father; then I will return.' "

After several days of waiting, some of the people in Pharaoh's court found the right time to speak to him about Joseph's request. They told him what Joseph had asked, then said, "O great king, please grant the request of your good servant Joseph, for you know how he loved his father."

And Pharaoh sent this message to Joseph: "Go up and bury your father, as he made you swear to do."

Joseph then made preparations to return to Canaan to bury his father. Pharaoh sent a huge delegation of his most important officials, all those from his own personal court and all the other officials of Egypt.

Besides all the Egyptians, of course all of Jacob's family went back with Joseph to Canaan. All the members of Joseph's household, all his brothers, and all of Jacob's own household went back to Canaan for Jacob's burial. They left only the youngest children in Egypt—everybody else made the trip back for the burial. Also, many chariots and riders on horseback made the trip, because Jacob was a very important man, and Pharaoh wanted to honor him with a large group of people at his funeral. They all gathered together and left for Canaan.

After many days of hot travel on the dusty roads on horses, on donkeys, and in chariots and wagons, the travelers reached Atad, a village near the Jordan River. When they reached the place where farmers threshed their wheat at Atad, Joseph and the others began to weep again for Jacob. So the group stopped there for seven days to hold a ceremony of mourning for Jacob. This village was in the land of Canaan, so the people there thought all these people coming up from Egypt were Egyptians—they didn't know that many of them had once lived in Canaan. So the local people renamed the place "Abel Mizraim," which in the Hebrew language means "mourning of the Egyptians." After seven days they left for Mamre.

They buried Jacob in the land of Canaan, as he had made Joseph swear to do. They brought him from Egypt into the land of Canaan and went to the village of Mamre. Near that village was the cave of Machpelah, which Jacob's grandfather Abraham had bought from the Hittite man named Ephron. Abraham bought the field near the cave, as well as the cave for a burial place, and Jacob's grandmother, grandfather, and both his parents were buried there. Canaan was the land that God had promised to Abraham, then to his son Isaac, and then again to Jacob. Jacob wanted to be buried in this Promised Land with his forefathers.

After they had buried Jacob in Canaan near Mamre, Joseph and his brothers and all the others went back to Egypt.

Once Joseph's brothers saw that Jacob was no longer around to protect them from Joseph, they became afraid. They thought it had only been because of their father that Joseph had not taken revenge on them before. So they made up a message, pretending that Jacob had said it before he died. They hoped that Joseph would honor his father's words. But Jacob never actually said it—the brothers just made it up. The message was, "This is what your father, Jacob, said: 'I ask you to forgive your brothers the sins and the wrongs they committed in treating you so badly.' Now please forgive the sins of the servants of the God of your father."

When Joseph heard what the brothers were trying to do, he was very sad that they were still afraid. He wanted them to know that they were forgiven already. Joseph wept.

Joseph's brothers then came to him and again bowed low to the ground before him, saying, "We are your slaves."

But Joseph replied, "Don't be afraid of me any longer. Am I in the place of God that I should take revenge on you for what you did? I know that you meant to do me evil, but God meant it for good, to accomplish what is now being done. Because I was here at the right time to make God's will known in the matter of the dream and the famine, many lives here in Egypt have been saved. So then, don't be afraid. I will provide for all of you and all your children."

Joseph made it very clear to his brothers that he had forgiven them for everything they had done. He spoke very kindly to all of them.

Joseph spent the rest of his life in Egypt, as a very important man and a servant and official under the king. He served in Pharaoh's court for many years and was greatly loved by all those in Pharaoh's household. He and his brothers saw each other and their families often and lived happily in Egypt. Pharaoh had given them the land of Goshen, one of the richest parts of Egypt. Goshen had green fields, rolling meadows full of grass for their cattle and sheep, and plenty of water. All Jacob's family did very well and were quite happy in their new home.

Joseph himself lived to be a hundred and ten years old. He lived so long that he got to see the births of his great-great-grandchildren, something very few people live to see.

Then one day, Joseph said to his brothers, many of whom had also lived to a great old age, "I am about to die. But God will surely come to your aid and take you up out of this land to the land He promised on oath to Abraham, Isaac, and Jacob."

Joseph then made his brothers, the sons of Israel, swear an oath to him. He told them, "God will surely come to your aid and bring you out of Egypt. And when He does, you must carry my bones up from this place." His brothers understood that Joseph was speaking about a much later time, and that he did not mean that they would be carrying his bones. Joseph knew that any promise his brothers made would be carried out by their descendants. So he asked his brothers, and they swore it to him.

In asking this of his brothers, Joseph was showing great faith in God. It takes a lot of faith to believe that something will happen many years after you will die! Yet Joseph knew that whatever the Lord promises, He will do! So Joseph gave instructions to his brothers and made them promise that their descendants would carry his bones with them back to the Promised Land whenever God led them back from Egypt.

Then Joseph died, at the ripe old age of a hundred and ten. The Egyptians and all his brothers held a long period of mourning for him, just as they had for his father, Jacob. And the Egyptians prepared his body for burial, a skill they had that the Hebrews did not have then. Finally, Joseph was buried in a coffin in Egypt.

Joseph had been a great man, and a man used mightily by the Lord. Why was Joseph, the son of Jacob, used by God to do mighty things for Him, like interpreting dreams and leading all of Egypt through a seven-year famine? Mostly, it was because Joseph had great faith in God. He believed that God was able and willing to help him and to protect him wherever he went, whether it was in a deep, dark cistern or a prison cell in a foreign country. He trusted God to take care of him even when it looked like things weren't going too well.

Joseph also knew it was very important to always do the right thing, even if it was not always the easy thing or the thing other people wanted him to do. Joseph knew that God expects us to try to be faithful to Him, just as He is always faithful to us.

And, as it turned out, Joseph was right when he said that God would bring Israel back out of Egypt and into the Promised Land. About four hundred years after Joseph died, an evil pharaoh rose up who did not remember Joseph and all the things he had done for Egypt. This pharaoh hated the people called Israelites and made them slaves. But God raised up another man, just as he raised up Joseph to take care of His people. This man, named Moses, did many miracles and led God's chosen people out from the land where they had become slaves. After many adventures and wandering around in the wilderness for forty years, the people of Israel came once again to the Promised Land, which they had left in Joseph's time, four hundred years before.

But before they left Egypt, Moses made sure the people of Israel went and got Joseph's bones out of the grave where they had been lying for so many years. Moses made sure that Joseph's bones were carried wherever they went as they wandered through the wilderness, even though it would have been easier to leave them behind. And finally, when the people of Israel entered the Promised Land, they carried Joseph's bones and laid them to rest with the graves of his family, just as he had wanted and as he had made his brothers swear so long ago. Joseph had known even then that the promise God had made to his great-grandfather Abraham, to his grandfather Isaac, and to his father, Jacob, would be kept. And God did keep His promise and made Israel a great nation in their land.

DAVID

THE WARRIOR KING

by Sam Wellman

CHAPTER 1

"Is that a lion?" blurted out young David.

He stopped strumming the small, nine-stringed harp he propped in his lap. Did he see a tawny form creeping from a ravine near his flock of sheep? He stood up. No, it was not a lion but a stray dog. He clapped his hands, and the dog bolted back up the ravine.

David's heart was beating hard. He trusted God, or thought he did. But was that trust great enough to allow him to face a lion? He picked up his harp and sang a psalm, an old sacred song that his father, Jesse, had taught him. It was said among the Jews the great Moses had written it. It began:

> Lord, you have been our dwelling place
> throughout all generations.
> Before the mountains were born
> or you brought forth the earth and the world,
> from everlasting to everlasting you are God.
>
> You turn men back to dust,
> saying, "Return to dust, O sons of men."
> For a thousand years in your sight
> are like a day that has just gone by.*

---

*Psalm 90:1–4

It was a long song, but David sang the whole thing. He was very good at remembering the exact words of songs, as well as the words of the five sacred books of Moses.

The life of a shepherd boy could be lonely. Wise boys used their time alone in the fields to grow stronger. David was fifteen, and he made the most of being by himself. He prayed to Almighty God, often composing his prayers as poetry. Then he sang his prayers while he strummed the strings on his harp.

Apparently he played well. When he was allowed to join his family in Bethlehem, even his older brothers listened to him. Usually they didn't want to hear what he had to say and told him to be quiet. But David's oldest brother, Eliab, and two more of his seven brothers were soldiers in King Saul's army, so they were rarely at home anyway.

"But they are at home now," reflected David.

He wished he were there, but the sheep had to be tended. He rose and stowed his precious harp inside the small hut he slept in. It was covered by heavy mats of goat hair, woven by the women of his family. The grass-carpeted hills where David shepherded his father's sheep were rocky with scrubby bushes.

Like all shepherds, David carried a staff and a heavy club called a rod. He used the staff to prod stubborn sheep, although most came willingly to his call. His heavy club was used to strike unwelcome intruders. Usually, though, the intruders—like wolves or hyenas—were too far away to hit with a club. Then he had to drive them away with a well-placed shot from his sling. He practiced using his sling as much as he did his harp.

"It is a well-known sacred story that among the ancient Jewish armies there were seven hundred Benjamites who could sling a stone at a hair and not miss," David reminded himself (Judges 20:16). "But many have forgotten how deadly this skill is."

David belonged to the tribe of Judah—one of the twelve Jewish tribes descended from the patriarchs Abraham, Isaac, and Jacob. Jacob lived about one thousand years before David. Moses, the great Jewish prophet who took the Jewish tribes out of slavery in Egypt, lived about five hundred years before David.

The Benjamites, the Jewish tribe famous for their skill with slingshots, were neighbors to David's tribe of Judah. King Saul was a Benjamite. He had united many of the Jewish tribes. Many people thought of him as the first Jewish king. That was why David's older brothers fought for him.

"There is another reason I practice with my sling," he murmured as he selected some rounded, egg-sized rocks. "The day may come when an intruder will not run away."

David could scarcely bring himself to think of what that would be like. Every once in awhile, his father and his brothers had warned him, a lion wandered up from the valley of the Jordan River far to the east. David had seen a dead lion once. It had been old, desperate for easy prey. David couldn't imagine facing such a huge beast—old or young—with such enormous daggers for claws and ferocious spikes for teeth.

Large brown bears lived in the rocky recesses of these highlands. Bears, too, were known to try to take a sheep from time to time. Yes, some day David might have to fight such terrors as these—all alone with nothing but his club and a sling. So he had a very good reason to practice with his sling.

As he hurled rocks with such speed that they hummed through the air, he thought of another song:

They have tracked me down,
they now surround me,
with eyes alert, to throw me to the ground.
They are like a lion hungry for prey,
like a great lion crouching in cover.*

But why stop his poem at the danger? Why not appeal to God, Whom David loved so much?

Rise up, O LORD, confront them,
bring them down;
rescue me from the wicked by your sword.†

Jewish poetry did not rhyme; it was written in couplets or pairs of lines. The second line usually used different words

---

*Psalm 17:11–12
†Psalm 17:13

to repeat the thought in the first line. David had composed thousands of couplets in his days as a shepherd.

"David!" boomed a voice in the air. A man walked across the grassy slope. He was dressed like David, with a long heavy cloak flapping over a simple light tunic. Of course his clothes were made of wool. Except for leather sandals, would the sons of Jesse wear anything but wool? It was one of David's brothers. David's brother yelled, "You must go home right away. Father wants you!"

"But what of the sheep?"

"I'm to watch them until you return."

"But why am I being called?"

"Just obey!" snapped the brother. "Go! Run, little brother!"

David loped across the hillsides. Was someone sick at home? His father, Jesse, wasn't sick, was he? Maybe not. David's brother said it was his father who wanted him. Still, David's father was no longer young. Nor was David's mother. Perhaps she was sick. After all, she had given birth to more than ten children.

David's heart pounded as he saw the walled town of Bethlehem in the distance. Outside the walls lived most of the men who ran large flocks of sheep and goats. Some lived in sturdy goat hair tents; some lived in simple mud-brick houses. David steeled himself and walked onto his father's property.

"God, let this problem be small," he prayed.

Outside Jesse's drab brick house was a bouquet of color from many large tents draped with dyed hides. The floors of the tents were covered with elegant floral carpets. A big crowd of people, including all the elders, were gathered there.

David's heart sang when he saw his father sitting by the main residence. Jesse seemed in full health. And there was his mother standing with David's sisters. Praise God she was all right. Now David saw that a calf was being sacrificed to God. A man David didn't know was seated with his father and the elders. The stranger looked to be about eighty years old. His robe was as fine as any David had ever seen.

The old man rose suddenly. "So this is the one!" he cried in surprise, looking up as if speaking to no one but God. He directed his attention to David. "You are indeed a handsome young fellow. Strong and healthy looking."

"God be with you, Sir," answered David, bowing.

"Kneel," said the old man. "I am to anoint you."

David saw the old man take a horn encased on both ends by bright yellow metal. The metal seemed too bright, too yellow for brass. Could it be gold? The old man poured oil from the horn into his hand.

David inhaled the oil's sharp, spicy fragrances. Many fragrances were in the fine oil. Was that myrrh he smelled? Some delicious scents he could not identify. Was one the famous spikenard? Who was this very important old man? David felt the warm oil soak into his hair. The old man's gentle hands spread it over his head.

Suddenly David no longer wondered about what was happening. The Holy Spirit entered him. Never had David felt so fearless and so full of peace.

The old man left abruptly. Then David got up.

"Who was he?" David asked his father.

Father Jesse seemed in shock. "He said he was Samuel from Ramah."

"The great prophet Samuel!" gasped all the brothers at the same time.

CHAPTER 2

"Yes, he said he was Samuel," said one of the elders.

"I saw Samuel years ago," said another elder. "That old man didn't look like Samuel to me."

"I also saw Samuel once," said another. "I believe the old man was Samuel."

"But why was he here?" asked the oldest brother, Eliab.

"I don't know," answered Jesse.

"Perhaps to anoint a king," gasped one of the elders.

"Nonsense!" said Eliab angrily. "Samuel has already anointed a king. Saul is our king. I'll bet the old man was an imposter."

"He didn't look like an imposter," said David.

"Oh, be quiet," snarled Eliab. "Go back to your sheep, you pup."

His father gave David a puzzled look. "Yes, Son, it is best that you return to the flock."

So David returned to the sheep without telling anyone the glorious feeling he had as the rich oil was put on his head. Was it truly the Spirit of God Who had entered him? David believed that it was. He also believed God did everything for a purpose. Did David's anointing somehow mean he would soon be put to a test?

"Whatever happens, I will trust the Lord," he promised.

In the winter, the sheep were brought down from the heights to graze very close to Bethlehem. But summer had not reached its peak yet, so David gradually worked the sheep higher into the hills. Some of the wild creatures in the hot lowlands sought the coolness of the heights, too. Hyenas, wolves, and bears roamed the hills, so David was always on the alert. His flock was full of young lambs. A shepherd had to defend every sheep, every lamb, just as Almighty God—the great shepherd—defended His people.

David put that thought into a new song:

The LORD is my strength and my shield;
my heart trusts in him, and I am helped.
My heart leaps for joy and I will give
thanks to him in song.

The LORD is the strength of his people,
a fortress of salvation for his anointed one.
Save your people and bless your inheritance;
*be their shepherd and carry them forever.**

One day, as David made his rounds of the sheep, he heard a low rumble. It was the most horrible sound he had ever heard. It was as if the very earth were growling as it supposedly did in earthquakes. Yet this awful sound was not from the rocks. David had never heard the sound before, but he knew what it came from.

---

*Psalm 28:7–9

"A lion," he gulped.

David gently placed his staff and heavy cloak on the grassy slope. He unslung his weighty club. The club was made from oak. It had a knot on the end as hard as iron. But it had never been called on to do what it might have to do this day.

David crouched down and crept toward the blood-chilling sound. Yes, there was the source. Not fifty yards away in a dry ravine stood a great male lion with a mane as black as a tomb! The lion had its paw on a lamb. The sound the lion had made was not a warning. It was a rumbling of pleasure. For the lion was absorbed in its tiny victim. The lamb bleated. The poor little creature was still alive. It cried for its shepherd David's mercy.

"God, in Your great mercy, grant me strength," prayed David.

David felt power explode inside himself. He burst toward the lion. Never had he run so fast. The lion still had not seen him. David leaped the last dozen feet, swinging the club as he flew through the air. As he landed in the sand of the ravine, he brought the club down with all his might. The lion's skull whomped like a great melon. The lion snarled in anger and staggered away from the lamb. David saw blood on the lamb's white wool. He was angry at what the lion had done to the poor lamb.

Groggily, the lion turned on David. Its yellow eyes were glazed. David hammered the club down on its skull again.

He leaped on the lion. Grabbing its thick black mane, he hammered its skull again and again with his club.

Finally the lion was dead. David saw the lamb rise and steady itself on wobbly legs. Then it stumbled off to find its mother. Soon it was skipping around her as if nothing had happened.

The anger David had felt drained away. Never had David felt such anger. Had he done right? Was anger in itself a sin? No, David decided. Anger was wrong only if it led to sin.

"God allowed me to kill the lion in order to save the lamb," he said in amazement. "Praise God for His mercy and wisdom."

David's great moment had not happened at all the way he had imagined it. He had dreamed he would interrupt the lion's kill. He would clap his hands. The lion would stand and face him. Then David would hurl a stone with his sling. The stone would bury itself in the lion's skull. The lion would fall dead.

"God had a different plan," he admitted.

David did not boast of his triumph to anyone. He had killed the lion with God's help.

The next summer, David killed a vicious rogue of a brown bear. It, too, was in the process of killing a lamb. David beat the bear to death with his stout club. He knew that God helped him protect the sheep.

One day, David got a visit from one of his brothers. The brother sighed. "You are to go back to father in Bethlehem.

I'll stay with the sheep. Take your harp."

"Am I to attend religious services?" asked David.

"Just go, little brother. Obey."

David was used to being called home to attend services in a tent tabernacle or to be instructed in religion. The Jews in his day studied the five books of Moses: Genesis, Exodus, Leviticus, Numbers, and Deuteronomy. In these books were the Ten Commandments as well as many other laws.

Even the tabernacle and its courtyard had to be constructed exactly as described by Moses. The courtyard had to have north and south sides of one hundred cubits. A cubit was about one and a half feet, so these sides were about 150 feet long. The west and east sides of the courtyard were fifty cubits, or about seventy-five feet long. The courtyard was surrounded by curtains of finely twisted linen that hung from a specific number of posts with bronze bases and silver hooks. The curtains were five cubits high, or about seven and a half feet.

People entered the courtyard only on the east side. In the open courtyard was a bronze altar where offerings were burned.

"I offered a young pigeon once," remembered David.

The actual tabernacle—the place for worship and thinking about the presence of God—was thirty cubits by ten cubits, or about forty-five feet by fifteen feet. The tabernacle had a wooden framework covered with linen and animal hides. One room held the seven-branched candle stand called a menorah, the altar where incense was burned, and a table for "show-bread"—one loaf from each of the twelve Jewish tribes.

Behind a veil of blue, scarlet, and purple linen embroidered with cherubim was the second room, called the Most Holy Place. It housed the Ark of the Covenant, a chest that contained the five books of Moses and the actual stone tablets with the Ten Commandments.

The lid of the chest was called the Mercy Seat. On each end of the lid stood golden cherubim—angels with outstretched wings and heads bowed toward the Mercy Seat.

The Most Holy Place was entered only once a year and only by the high priest. Although Jews worshiped and brought sacrifices to many tabernacles, only one tabernacle had the actual Ark of the Covenant. David's father told him that this tabernacle was in the town of Kiriath-jearim, about fifteen miles northwest of Bethlehem.

As David hurried from the fields to Bethlehem, he wondered if he had forgotten one of the holy feast days of the Jews. But it was summer. The only feast day observed in summer was the Feast of the Harvest. At the Feast of the Harvest, special consideration was given to widows, drifters, children, servants, and the fatherless. These less-privileged Jews feasted that day. The Feast of the Harvest came at the same time as the wheat harvest. David's father had a small wheat field. So David could hardly have forgotten such an important feast day. Why did his father want to see him?

When David arrived in Bethlehem, his father, Jesse, was

standing with a soldier. Jesse looked worried.

"Did something bad happen to one of my brothers?" David blurted out.

Jesse said to David, "King Saul is looking for a good harp player. Your brother Eliab told him about you. You are to go to King Saul's camp with this soldier. But I want you to take gifts to the king."

So David left Bethlehem with a goat and a donkey loaded with bread and wine. King Saul lived in the Benjamite stronghold of Gibeah, about six miles north of Bethlehem. But David already knew from his older brothers' movements that King Saul was rarely there from springtime through fall. He was usually camped somewhere in the countryside, fighting neighboring nations.

All the Jews especially disliked the Philistines, a hostile people far to the west. The Philistines had mastered the art of making iron weapons. They even had great iron war chariots pulled by mighty warhorses. So only up in the rugged highlands—where the chariots were useless—did the Jews dare to oppose the Philistines.

The soldier led David to King Saul's camp in one of these rugged river valleys to the west. David was rushed to the king's oversized, luxurious tent.

"Play!" ordered King Saul.

"Hurry," urged an attendant. "The king has a ferocious headache."

King Saul was about fifty-five years old, but he towered

a full head above everyone around him. He paced the carpeted floor of his tent, great purple robes flying behind him. His face would have been very handsome if pain had not distorted it so much. It seemed as if a knife were stuck in his skull.

David felt the Spirit of the Lord as he began strumming the strings of his harp. He knew just the song to sing. He smiled at King Saul as he played. Yes, David would soothe this anguished king:

> *We will shout for joy when you are victorious and*
> *will lift up our banners in the name of our God.*
> *May the LORD grant all your requests.*
>
> *Now I know that the LORD saves his anointed;*
> *he answers him from his holy heaven with the*
> *saving power of his right hand.*
>
> *Some trust in chariots and some in horses,*
> *but we trust in the name of the LORD our God.*
> *They are brought to their knees and fall,*
> *but we rise up and stand firm.*
>
> *O LORD, save the king!*
> *Answer us when we call!**

---

*Psalm 20:5–9

Pain melted off King Saul's face until he actually returned David's smile.

"You sing like an angel," the king said. Suddenly he barked, "Enough for now! The pain is gone. You'll do."

He turned to an attendant. "Put this boy in the tent with my armor bearers. Teach him how to serve me in that way, too."

David could see King Saul did not really look at him. David was invisible to the king. Over the next weeks, David learned the story of Saul. The story really began with the great prophet Samuel. Samuel was also a judge. For hundreds of years the Jews had been ruled by judges and had tried to live in peace with their neighboring nations. They fought only to protect themselves.

When Samuel grew old, his sons were too corrupt to become the next judges. The people demanded a king. Samuel warned them that a king would make great demands on them. A king would not only tax them but would also take their sons into his army to start wars against neighbors. The people insisted they did not care. They wanted to be part of a powerful nation. God was angry that the Jews rejected peaceful ways.

But later God told Samuel, "I have heard the call of the people. You must anoint as first king the son of the Benjamite Kish."

One day Samuel saw Saul, the son of Kish. Saul was taller and more handsome than any other man among the Jews. Sure that this young man should be king, Samuel anointed him.

And indeed, the Spirit of the Lord entered Saul.

Yet Saul had great doubts. He wasn't sure that he could be a good king. When the day came that Samuel announced Saul was to be the first king, Saul was hiding. But Saul still became the king. Many Jews doubted him and made fun of him. Saul knew nothing about being a king. The first time the people asked him to defend them—against invading Ammonites—Saul was plowing a field with his oxen!

But the Spirit of the Lord filled Saul with courage. Saul rallied the Jews and attacked the Ammonites still sleeping in their tents. Not only were the Jews surprised that they were now victorious fighters, but all their enemies were surprised, too. Everyone knew that the Jews did not have blacksmiths who could make swords and spears. The Jews even had to buy their plows from other nations.

With his son, Jonathan, also commanding an army, King Saul was soon defending the Jewish highlands against every nation around them, even the very powerful Philistines. But Saul was a very troubled man. During a big battle, he did not obey God's instructions. Then he lied to Samuel about what he had done.

God told Samuel to tell Saul that He would find another king for the Jews. From that day on, Samuel never visited Saul again. All this happened years before the time David joined King Saul's camp to play the harp for him. By then, King Saul was often unhappy and had very bad headaches.

David often wondered about Samuel. *If Samuel were here*

now, I would know if he was the one who anointed me.

Often David was allowed to return to his home in Bethlehem to help Jesse with his sheep. This usually happened when Saul was in good health. When his headaches returned, David was summoned.

One day, David was told to go to Saul's camp for a different reason. He was called from his flock long before dawn. David could guess his mission when he saw his father standing by a donkey loaded with provisions.

Jesse said, "Take this sack of roasted grain and ten loaves of bread to your three brothers in King Saul's camp." Jesse winked. "Give these blocks of cheese to the commander of their unit."

"But where is the camp now, Sir?"

"They are in the valley of the Elah River, between the villages of Socoh and Azekah."

David quickly found the upper reaches of the Elah and trudged down the valley. The Elah flowed straight west and emptied into the Mediterranean Sea. Only one enemy would be in that valley: the Philistines.

When David reached Saul's sprawling camp on one side of the Elah, the air rang with war cries. The great armies were taking their positions. David quickly found the unit of his brothers, Eliab, Abinadab, and Shammah.

The Jewish army of King Saul faced an equally sprawling Philistine army across the valley. In the hilly uplands where the Philistines could not take their thousands of horse-drawn war chariots, the Jews could fight them toe to toe. David had barely spoken to his three brothers when the ranks of soldiers began buzzing with alarm.

"There he is—again!" groaned one. "This disgrace to the Jews has been going on for forty days!"

David looked down in the valley. Advancing from the Philistines was one soldier and his armor bearer. The Philistine warrior wore a helmet and a great coat of scaled armor, all of golden bronze. His legs were protected by bronze plates, too. On his back was a great spear. Clutched in his hand was a gleaming sword. The armor bearer struggled to carry the warrior's shield.

"I can't believe my eyes," gasped David. "The Philistine warrior must be nine feet tall!"

CHAPTER 3

"He must be part of the race of giants from Gath," murmured David.

"Listen to the little know-it-all," one Jewish soldier snapped bitterly at David. The voice sounded like that of David's oldest brother, Eliab.

The valley boomed with the giant's voice. "Why do you Jewish cowards come out and line up for battle? Am I—Goliath—not a Philistine? Are you not soldiers of Saul? Choose one man to come down here and fight me!" The valley rumbled with the giant's laugh. "If your man defeats me, then we Philistines will serve Saul. But if I win, you must serve us!"

"Who will go?" wondered David aloud.

"I defy you Jewish cowards and your phony God!" taunted Goliath.

How dare the giant defy Almighty God! David waited for the champion of the Jews to walk down in the valley and face the giant Goliath. Jewish soldiers were stirring, but they weren't full of determination and anger. They were full of fear. A few even became so unnerved that they ran back up into the hills. David could not believe what he was hearing and seeing.

"You would think some poor fool would take Goliath

on," grumbled one Jewish soldier. "After all, King Saul is offering his champion not only his daughter in marriage but a fortune, as well."

"King Saul is offering all that?" asked David in surprise.

David's oldest brother, Eliab, became furious. "Be quiet. We all know how good you think you are. Why have you come here, anyway? Why don't you go back to your handful of sheep!"

"Can't I even speak?" sighed David.

But he knew why Eliab and the others were so touchy. Goliath made them all feel like cowards. And his taunting had been going on for forty days! The entire Jewish army was being disgraced. There was not one man who would face the giant for King Saul. Suddenly David knew the Spirit of God was moving him to act. He slipped away to the grand tent that was King Saul's. As he expected, King Saul was not in a good mood.

"If only I were younger!" growled Saul, "but I'm almost sixty years old now. I can't fight a giant in his prime."

"Perhaps I can help, Your Majesty," volunteered David.

"Who are you, Boy?" asked King Saul, startled.

"I often play the harp for you," answered David, who knew King Saul never actually saw him.

"What do you want? I didn't send for you to play the harp for me. I don't have a headache, but I should!"

"No Jew should lose heart this day, Your Majesty. I will fight the Philistine."

Saul groaned. "Don't be ridiculous. You are a boy. Goliath has been a warrior for many years."

"I may seem a boy, Your Majesty, but I have killed a lion and a bear." David knew that at last it was time to tell of his success with the wild beasts.

"A lion? A bear?" Saul seemed to see David for the first time. "You are telling the truth, aren't you?"

"Just as the living God protected me from those great raging beasts, He will protect me from this giant."

"God protects you?" King Saul was excited now. "Put my armor on this champion of the Jews!" he cried.

But Saul's spirits sagged again as he saw David struggle under the weight of the king's massive armor. David could scarcely lift Saul's sword. Saul was speechless as David removed the armor and walked out of the tent. Numbly the king followed to watch.

"Maybe David's death will make one of my real soldiers want to fight Goliath," grumbled the king.

David carried only his staff and his sling. He paused in a dry creek bed on his way down into the valley and selected five smooth, egg-sized stones. Then he continued into the valley to face the giant.

The giant smiled. At last he would be able to kill some Jewish fool. David knew he must be thinking David was an armor bearer for the Jewish champion. Eventually Goliath shrugged and frowned. Where was the Jewish soldier? Then he must have noticed the fire in David's eyes.

"What!" screamed Goliath. "Am I a dog that you cowardly Jews throw me sticks?"

"You come against me with sword and spear," cried David, "but I come against you in the name of the Almighty God!"

"Come on then with your phony God!" yelled Goliath angrily. "I will soon throw your dead carcass to the buzzards and the jackals!"

David yelled as loud as he could, "Today I will prove the God of the Jews is real and living!"

"Enough of your silliness," growled Goliath, and he began to advance on David. He balanced the spear that he intended to hurl through David.

David, full of the Spirit of the Lord, calmly placed one of his perfect stones in the pocket of his sling. Like the Benjamites, he could hit a hair fifty feet away. Goliath was that close now. David twirled the sling until it hummed like a thousand angry hornets. He let one end of the sling go. The stone blurred straight to its target. *Whack!* Goliath blinked and toppled forward. The earth shuddered. Was he dead or just stunned?

David never knew himself—nor did anyone else— because within seconds he had dashed over to draw Goliath's own great sword from its scabbard. In spite of its enormous weight, David had the strength to heft it high in the air. He swung it thundering down into the giant's exposed neck.

"What is that deafening roar?" said David, looking up.

The hillsides had erupted. Both armies were screaming

and moving. The Philistines had panicked and were running toward the main road to their home. The Jews fell upon them, at last fighting like true soldiers of the Almighty God.

Abner, King Saul's cousin and his greatest general, came to David. He told David to bring the severed head of Goliath to King Saul. That was the custom in those days. It proved that the enemy was truly destroyed. David could barely carry the giant's heavy head. It was displayed in King Saul's tent.

"Look!" roared King Saul. "Buried deep in the giant's forehead is David's stone!"

King Saul was delighted. His son Jonathan was especially pleased with this champion for the Jews, David from Beth-lehem. His eyes seemed to recognize David as one of God's chosen heroes. First, Jonathan put his own tunic on David, then his belt, his sword, his bow, even his robe! King Saul seemed less pleased with David with each generous gift from Jonathan.

But then Jonathan stunned everyone. "I swear my friend-ship to David in the name of the Lord!"

David was filled with joy. "And I swear my friendship to you in the name of the Lord!"

When Jonathan and David pledged everlasting friendship to each other as a sacred covenant with the Lord, David could see King Saul had to fight becoming angry. Saul was a very handsome man, and the slightest anger soured his face. David knew only too well that Saul could change from happiness to rage in seconds. So David left the king's presence.

The hillsides were alive with activity. After the Jewish army plundered the Philistine camp, King Saul led it back through the highlands toward Gibeah. Crowds of Jews greeted them everywhere. The soldiers told them of David's heroism.

Women danced among the triumphant warriors and played music on tambourines and small three-stringed harps called lutes. In exuberant joy they sang over and over again:

"Saul has slain his thousands,
*and David his tens of thousands."**

David heard that King Saul was offended. David was too popular in Saul's mind. Now when Saul looked at David, the young harpist was no longer invisible. David had become an object of suspicion, perhaps even of loathing.

I must watch the king as carefully as he watches me, David warned himself.

The next day David was summoned to play the harp for King Saul. This was at King Saul's palace in Gibeah. The large palace was fine for its day, built not of mud bricks but of rounded cobbles carefully selected from the beds of streams. The interior of the stone fortress was softened by many beautiful drapes and carpets. King Saul and his court lounged on cushions while David strummed the harp and sang:

---

*1 Samuel 18:7

O LORD, our Lord,
how majestic is your name in all the earth!

You have set your glory
above the heavens.
From the lips of children and infants
you have ordained praise
because of your enemies,
to silence the foe and the avenger.

When I consider your heavens,
the work of your fingers,
the moon and the stars,
which you have set in place,
what is man that you are mindful of him,
the son of man that you care for him?*

David noticed the king's handsome face became more and more troubled. If King Saul would only be patient, he would soon know David's song would confirm his right to rule.

"I must rid myself of this nuisance!" the king suddenly shrieked, and he threw a spear.

King Saul's spear came straight at David!

David dodged that spear and a second spear. Then he

---

*Psalm 8:1–4

dashed off through the many rooms of the palace. He would avoid King Saul until the man calmed down. Surely, reasoned David, the king was momentarily out of his head.

What happened after that seemed to prove it.

"I'm putting you in command of one thousand soldiers," said King Saul to David later, as if nothing had happened. "I want you to campaign against my enemies in the countryside."

So David took the men out in the country. He suspected King Saul thought this would expose him as a mere shepherd boy who knew nothing about soldiering. But Jonathan, who was a very experienced general, advised David on how to command. And David, who knew the Jewish highlands well —every hill, every forest, every cave—did well with his one thousand soldiers.

Rarely were he and his thousand surprised by an attack. Often they fell upon encampments of invading enemy soldiers. Although fighting put blood on David's hands, he was sure God allowed men to fight invaders of the Jews, just as surely as God allowed the shepherd to fight the predators of sheep. He and his men triumphed over many invaders.

Months later, David was summoned by King Saul. He was still hailed as a hero. Now he had even more triumphs to his name.

"You seem to have forgotten I promised my daughter to the victor over Goliath," said Saul, unable to disguise his dislike. "Now I offer you my daughter Michal."

"But I don't deserve to be the king's son-in-law," answered David.

King Saul didn't seem to know how to take David's refusal. Was David truly modest? Or was he slighting his daughter? The terrible-tempered, unpredictable King Saul let it pass.

Soon the king learned that his daughter Michal actually loved David. Again he offered his daughter to David. How could David refuse now?

But Jonathan warned David that the king might not be doing it because he wanted to honor his daughter's wishes. David again modestly told the king he did not deserve to be his son-in-law. This time the king did not accept his refusal.

"The only price you must pay me for my treasure of a daughter is triumph over the Philistines," said King Saul.

Then the king asked David to conquer the Philistines down in the plain. There they were virtually invincible in their chariots. David suspected that the king intended to send him to his death. But David was sure God was with him, so he did as the king asked. This time David was the invader, but he reasoned he was doing the bidding of his king. And this king had been anointed by Samuel on orders from God.

When David returned after defeating the Philistines in several battles, Saul arranged the wedding. A wedding was a great occasion, especially for a princess. Michal waited at the palace. Her face was covered with a veil, and she wore a richly embroidered white gown. Dressed in elegant robes given to him by Jonathan, David arrived, accompanied by his family and friends. His procession also included musicians, singers, and dancers.

In a short ceremony, King Saul gave his daughter Michal to David. Then the married couple left for the house David had rented in Gibeah. All the way the procession danced and celebrated.

At the house, the celebration continued. Guests were feasted and entertained for no less than seven days!

King Saul seemed more upset than ever. Everything always seemed to turn out in David's favor. Jonathan told David his father was now convinced God had chosen David to become the next king. Saul might never accept David as his successor. In fact, Saul might be asking men to kill David.

Jonathan urged David to go into hiding until he could find out for sure if his father planned to kill David. When Jonathan returned to David, he told him his father had assured him he was not angry at all. He even wanted David to play his harp for him again. So David played.

Once again King Saul was seized by a fit. "Take this, you upstart!" he screamed.

David ducked just in time to avoid the spear Saul threw at him. He left the palace. When he reached his own house, David was not particularly worried because King Saul's fits came and went. But this time Michal, David's wife and Saul's daughter, urged him to hide.

"Men are watching the house," she cried. "They have

been ordered to kill you in the morning!"

David lowered himself out a back window and escaped. Hiding in the countryside, he composed a song about his narrow escape:

Deliver me from my enemies, O God;
protect me from those who rise up against me.
Deliver me from evildoers
and save me from bloodthirsty men.
See how they lie in wait for me!
Fierce men conspire against me
for no offense or sin of mine, O LORD.
I have done no wrong,
yet they are ready to attack me.
*Arise to help me; look on my plight!**

This time David went to Ramah to see the great prophet Samuel. Samuel was very old, but David recognized him as the man who had anointed him. So David knew at last that God had chosen him for some great mission. He told Samuel that King Saul was trying to kill him. Samuel told David to stay with him.

Every time men arrived from King Saul to harm David, they were changed by the Spirit of the Lord. They joined Samuel and David to sing and dance in the joy of the Lord. Finally,

---

*Psalm 59:1–4

King Saul himself arrived. The Spirit of the Lord seized him, too. He threw away his elegant royal robes and rejoiced!

But David could not stay under Samuel's protection forever. Besides, David wanted his freedom. He went to Jonathan.

"Your father is still trying to kill me," he told Jonathan.

"Kill you? Never! My father tells me everything, and he never lies to me."

"Perhaps once that was true. But since you pledged your loyalty to me, he has not trusted you."

Jonathan trusted David completely. "How can I help you?"

"I'm supposed to join your father at his palace in Gibeah for the feast for the New Moon. But I fear a trap. I'll hide in the area until you find out what he intends to do. Meanwhile, you can say you gave me permission to go to Bethlehem to be with my family. If he becomes extremely angry, I believe it will be because he planned to trap me."

Jonathan devised a plan to let David know what he found out about his father's intentions. David was to hide behind a boulder in a field beyond the palace. Jonathan would shoot arrows into the field and send a small boy to fetch them. If he yelled, "No, they are closer this way!" it would mean David could come into the royal court safely. But if Jonathan yelled, "No, they are farther beyond!" David must flee far beyond the royal court and the town of Gibeah.

At the agreed-upon time, David hid behind the boulder. Then he heard Jonathan's cry. "No, they are farther beyond!" Now even Jonathan knew the truth! King Saul did want to kill David. David stepped out from his hiding place and bowed in appreciation to Jonathan three times. He could see Jonathan was filled with shame over his father's sick rage. Jonathan renewed his pledge of loyalty to David.

"Go in peace," he yelled to David, "for the Lord is our witness that we will be friends forever."

But without food or weapons or soldiers, David had never been in a more desperate situation.

CHAPTER 4

It was now clear to David that King Saul wanted him dead. David certainly could not enter the nearby fortress city of Jerusalem. It was held by the Jebusites, who were enemies of the Jews. So David fled to Nob, a village south of King Saul's Gibeah and east of Jerusalem.

Although Nob did not have the Ark of the Covenant, it had the main Jewish tabernacle and many priests. There David could seek God's guidance. David was hungry, too.

Ahimelech, the high priest in Nob, had only showbread, the bread consecrated to God. However, he allowed David to eat the bread. The high priest also gave David a sword.

In Nob, David noticed the Edomite Doeg, one of King Saul's servants. Doeg would surely go report his whereabouts to King Saul, but David did not harm him.

I must go far away from the Jewish highlands, realized David.

His desperate flight west took him down into the coastal plain among the Philistines. Even though he was older and now wore a beard, he was recognized as the Jew who had killed Goliath of Gath. As he was dragged before the king of Gath, David heard from his captors that he would surely be killed. He was a man far too dangerous to let live.

David pretended to be crazy, barking and whinnying,

letting his saliva drool onto his beard. The king of Gath was alarmed. Who knew if this craziness might spread?

"Why bring him to me?" the king shouted. "Am I short of madmen? Get him out of my palace!"

David would find no refuge from King Saul among the Philistines. Now he fled to some caves near Adullam, up in the Jewish highlands. This refuge was about halfway between the main strongholds of King Saul and the Philistines. In the cave he composed songs, as he always did, to praise the Almighty. Part of his composition about his narrow escape in Gath said:

> The righteous cry out, and the LORD hears them;
> he delivers them from all their troubles.

> The LORD is close to the brokenhearted and saves
> those who are crushed in spirit.

> A righteous man may have many troubles, but the
> LORD delivers him from them all; he protects all his
> bones, not one of them will be broken.*

David's years as a shepherd boy in the highlands served him well now. For David had always been a careful observer. Now he knew where to find food in the wild. Not every animal and plant could be eaten.

---

*Psalm 34:17–20

The Law of Moses was specific. No warm-blooded, four-legged animal could be eaten unless it had split hooves and chewed a cud. That meant a Jew could eat only certain wild deer, antelopes, and goats. Fortunately, David knew their favorite places.

Edible birds were also defined under the Law of Moses. Birds that gripped food in their claws were as a rule forbidden. But that still allowed David to eat partridges, doves, and waterfowl. David also knew where these could be found.

No reptiles could be eaten, but all scaled fish were allowed. In addition, a person who knew the wilderness could find fruit, roots, locusts, and honey to eat.

"I can survive very well by myself," admitted David. "God provides."

But he missed his wife, Michal. Would he ever see her again? Soon David was joined by his father, Jesse, and his brothers. His brothers no longer regarded him as the know-it-all little brother but as a mighty warrior. They knew now that Samuel's visit to Bethlehem heralded a great destiny for David.

Over the next weeks, many men who were angry with King Saul joined David. When David had four hundred men, he took his father and mother east across the Jordan River into the lowlands of Moab. There he intended to leave them with the king of Moab, who was an enemy of King Saul. Besides that, Jesse's grandmother, Ruth, the wife of Boaz, had been a Moabite. David even considered staying in

Moab himself. But Gad, a holy prophet traveling with David, objected.

"God wants you to go back to your Jewish highlands," insisted Gad.

So David went up into the Jewish highlands, into the forest of Hereth south of the caves of Adullam. Here he foraged a living among the bountiful game and fruits of the wild. He tried not to be discouraged, but what would ever become of him in this aimless, outlaw existence? Living off the countryside with four hundred followers was much more difficult.

One day his camp was joined by Abiathar, the son of the priest at Nob who had helped David. A terrible thing had happened. The Edomite Doeg had told King Saul about David's receiving help from the high priest. The high priest—Abiathar's father—and several other priests had been murdered. The king's regular soldiers refused to do it, so Doeg had performed the terrible acts himself.

David felt miserable. Could he have prevented the tragedy? But why was he blaming himself for King Saul's sinfulness? The fact that Saul's own soldiers had refused to obey the king meant the king was losing his influence.

"I must not give up," David said. "If men have been sacrificed for me, it is because God has some purpose for me."

David welcomed Abiathar into his band. Abiathar had also escaped with his father's ephod, the special vest the high priest wore over a blue robe when he served at the altar. Two onyx stones on the shoulders of the ephod were engraved with the names of the twelve Jewish tribes. The ephod brought by Abiathar made David realize even more what he owed to God and to God's chosen people, the Jews.

David and his men always helped fellow Jews when they could. Philistines raided Keilah one summer to steal the precious wheat the people had just harvested. David prayed to God for guidance. God wanted David to help Keilah.

David rushed to Keilah with his tough warriors, now numbering six hundred. They routed the Philistines. Instead of stealing Keilah's wheat, the Philistines lost all their goods and livestock!

But David had to leave Keilah quickly. King Saul had heard what he had done and was leading his own army there to attack him. This time, David did not return to the forest of Hereth but moved his camp far south into the desert of Ziph. But he did not fool everyone in King Saul's court.

"Jonathan!" cried David.

"My father searches for you night and day," Jonathan ruefully admitted. "You must find a new refuge, but God will give you the strength to prevail."

Jonathan said he knew David was destined to be king. Although many thought Jonathan would succeed King Saul, Jonathan knew David would succeed his father. Jonathan said even his father knew David was destined to be king. Why then did King Saul pursue David? Because he had separated himself from God. The prophet Samuel had seen that separation many years earlier.

"I will gladly be second to you," Jonathan promised David before he left.

Jonathan's loyalty made David's difficult life easier to bear. By the time King Saul and his army stormed into the desert of Ziph, David and his men were in the neighboring desert of Maon. But King Saul pursued him there, too. David was saved a vicious battle with the king only because Saul was called back to defend one of his towns against invading Philistines.

Meanwhile, David moved his small army into the wilderness by the Dead Sea. An area there called En Gedi was full of caves. Men could live there a long time with sparkling fresh water from a spring and food from the wild goats. But if David thought he was free of Saul, he was mistaken. Soon Saul was back with his army of three thousand men, searching everywhere for David.

David and his army were hiding far back in an enormous cave near the Crags of the Wild Goats. One day, David could not believe his eyes. At the opening of the cave towered a man. The man peered into the inky blackness. He could not see what was in the cave. But David could see the man's crown plainly. The man was King Saul! Alone!

One of David's men whispered, "This is the day the Lord has delivered your enemy into your hands!"

"Kill him," muttered David's men.

"No, I will not kill King Saul," whispered David, "because

he is the Lord's anointed."

Yet David pulled a razor-sharp knife. He crept up to King Saul, who was now gazing down into the bright sunshine of the wilderness. With the knife, David sliced a corner off the king's elegant flowing robe. Then David withdrew into the blackness until King Saul left the cave. Then he ran after him.

"Your Majesty the King!" yelled David.

King Saul whirled to face him. "David!"

"Yes. Why do you listen to those who say I am your enemy? Just now I could have killed you in the cave. But I did not. And to prove I could have killed you, I cut off the corner of your robe!" David brandished the triangle of purple fabric.

"What is that you say?" King Saul pulled up the corners of his robe. When he saw that the triangle in David's hand was indeed from the corner of his purple robe, his face clouded. This time it was not in anger but shame and remorse.

"Once again you have bested me, David. You are more righteous than I am. You treat me well, but I treat you badly."

King Saul broke down, weeping.

When the king finally regained his composure, he said, "I know you will be the future king. I wish only that you spare my descendants and that you do not wipe my name from recorded history."

"I grant you that request gladly, Your Majesty."

King Saul left, his enormous height slumped in shame. But David remained with his band in the wilderness. Saul had a long history of changing his mind. David knew he could not trust the king to stay true to his word.

David was sorry to learn that the great prophet Samuel had died at Ramah. Would David ever fulfill the destiny that Samuel had promised by anointing him? It didn't seem so on some days.

"Meanwhile, I and my loyal followers must survive in the wilds," he vowed.

Near Carmel lived an extremely wealthy man named Nabal. David and his soldiers had often protected Nabal's vast herds of sheep and goats from marauders. But David had never met Nabal. So he sent emissaries to negotiate a meeting. Nabal sent them away with this insulting message: "Who is this David? Many servants run away from their masters these days!"

When David heard this, he was very angry. Refusing hospitality in the countryside was a great insult. So he left two hundred of his men behind with his belongings, and he marched with four hundred of his men toward Nabal's holdings. Before he could get there, he was met by a caravan. A well-dressed woman ran forward and threw herself down at David's feet.

"I am Abigail," cried the woman, "wife of Nabal. Please forgive my husband's offense against you."

Before David could answer, Abigail's servants had begun to treat him and his men to a feast. Her caravan also brought him gifts of two hundred loaves of bread, two great skins of wine, five huge sacks of roasted grain, one hundred delicious raisin cakes, and two hundred blocks of pressed figs.

Abigail told David wryly, "I pray that when you become the king of all the Jews, Sir, you will not have on your conscience the slaughter of the fool Nabal and his wife, Abigail. Perhaps you will even remember your lowly friend Abigail."

David liked Abigail very much. "Praise God for sending you to me," he said. She was not only wise but beautiful, too. Nevertheless she was married. So he continued, "No, I will do nothing to your husband, Nabal. Go home in peace."

After Abigail returned to her husband, Nabal had a stroke. Nabal was much older than Abigail and ate too much food. Within ten days he was dead.

When David heard that Nabal had died, he sent a proposal of marriage to Abigail. He prayed that this very wise woman would become his wife. When she arrived several days later, his heart leaped with joy. He had lost his first wife, Michal. After his escape from Gibeah several years before, King Saul had married her to another man. David had another wife named Ahinoam, whom he had married on one of his trips far to the north. Ahinoam was from Jezreel.

In those days, it was the custom of the Jewish people that if a man had enough wealth to support a large family, he could have more than one wife. But he was required to be faithful to his wives, and they to him.

One day, David learned that once again King Saul was on

the prowl. "He is sick in his mind again," muttered David.

This time King Saul was camped in the desert of Ziph. In the middle of the night with only Abishai, the son of David's sister Zeruiah, David sneaked into the king's huge encampment of three thousand soldiers. David recognized King Saul's oversized, luxurious tent and slipped inside. When Abishai saw King Saul lying among Abner and his other generals, he whispered to David, "Let me strike him dead."

"No," whispered David. "It is a sin to kill the Lord's anointed."

So Abishai watched in wonder as David took King Saul's spear and water jug, then slipped out of the tent. The two walked up a nearby hillside where David stood and cried out. Soon King Saul and the others stumbled groggily out of the tent. Hundreds of Saul's soldiers were now milling around.

"Who calls out?" yelled Abner.

"Abner, why didn't you guard your king?" taunted David and waved the king's spear and water jug.

"Is that you, David?" yelled the king.

"Yes, Your Majesty," answered David, "and why do you pursue me again? Did God command you to find me, or did men persuade you to search for me like a pesky flea that must be killed?"

King Saul realized that his spear in David's hand meant David once again could have killed him but had not. "Forgive my foolishness, David," he called, but he did not say why he kept following David.

Even after King Saul took his army north to Gibeah, David decided that staying in the Jewish uplands or the desert was too dangerous. For whatever reason, King Saul could never be trusted. So David went down on the coastal plain to live among the Philistines. King Saul would never attack David there.

Once the Philistine king became convinced David and his army would not attack him, he even gave them a town called Ziklag. The Philistine king knew David was a rebel hiding from King Saul. So he asked for David's help some day in the future when the Philistines attacked King Saul.

"You will see just what my army can do," answered David.

The Philistine king did not detect the double meaning of what David said.

CHAPTER 5

One year later, the Philistines marched to attack King Saul at Jezreel. David was in the rear of the army, but some of the Philistine commanders began to question the wisdom of his presence. Could this Jew be trusted to attack other Jews?

The Philistine king vouched for David, but the commanders insisted David and his army must leave. So David took his army back to Ziklag. He could not help King Saul now. Suddenly David forgot all about the fate of King Saul. As he approached his town of Ziklag, he saw that it had been attacked, plundered, and burned to the ground.

"Where are our women and children?" David asked one of the few survivors.

"They have been carried away by Amalekite raiders from the south."

David heard his men muttering against him. They were angry. Why had they gone with the Philistine king? They weren't wanted with the Philistine army anyway. In spite of his own grief, David asked Abiathar to bring him the ephod from Nob. He often wore it himself when he wanted God's guidance.

He prayed now for God's advice. God told him to pursue the raiders, so David left immediately. Far to the south, they came to a deep gorge called the Besor Ravine. Two hundred of David's men were too sick to go on. So David crossed the Besor Ravine with the rest of his men. Soon they found an Egyptian slave the Amalekite raiders had abandoned because he was too sick to travel. David nursed the slave back to health. The slave promised to take him to the village of the Amalekites.

Within days, David was returning to Ziklag. "This is now David's plunder," sang his men.

They had attacked the Amalekites and routed them. Many Amalekites escaped into the desert on camels. But David didn't care. He had his wives and children back, as well as all the other Jews taken from Ziklag. And he had a huge number of livestock and great wealth taken from the Amalekites.

When David and his army crossed the Besor Ravine, he picked up the rest of his men. The four hundred who went on the raid refused to share the Amalekite plunder with the two hundred who were too sick to continue.

But David intervened. "From this day forward, all in the army will share plunder, whether some are too sick to fight in the battle or not."

When he returned to Ziklag, he decided to share the wealth with more than his army. So David sent emissaries with gifts to Bethel, Ramoth Negev, and Jattir; to Aroer, Siphmoth, Eshtemoa, and Racal; to Hormah, Bor Ashan, Athach, and Hebron; to the Jerahmeelites and the Kenites; and to people in many other places where David and his men had camped. Not all of these recipients were Jews. Abigail agreed with his generosity, sure that David would be rewarded many times over in the future.

Emissaries told each group of town elders, "David sends you gifts from the plunder of the Lord's enemies."

But just three days after David returned to Ziklag, a tattered, beaten man stumbled into town with shocking news. The man was a soldier from King Saul's army. The Philistines David had been forced to leave had virtually annihilated King Saul's army on Mount Gilboa near Jezreel. King Saul was dead. Jews to the north were fleeing their villages. Worst of all, David's best friend, Jonathan, was dead. If only David had been with the Philistines, surely he could have saved Jonathan!

David mourned for days. His lament began:

Your glory, O Israel,
lies slain on your heights.
How the mighty have fallen!

Tell it not in Gath, proclaim it not in the streets of
*Ashkelon, lest the daughters of the Philistines be glad.**

Oh, how he would miss King Saul, in spite of his illness, and his son Jonathan:

---

*2 Samuel 1:19–20

Saul and Jonathan—
in life they were loved and gracious,
and in death they were not parted.
They were swifter than eagles,
*they were stronger than lions.**

But most of all he would miss his loyal friend:

I grieve for you, Jonathan my brother;
you were very dear to me.
Your love for me was wonderful.†

After a time of mourning, David asked God if he should travel to the north. God told him to go to Hebron. There David was anointed king of the house of Judah. He also learned at Hebron that a few Jews from Jabesh Gilead in the Jordan Valley had managed to rescue the bodies of King Saul and Jonathan from the wall in Beth Shan where they had been displayed by the Philistines. In Jabesh Gilead, the rescuers burned the bodies of King Saul and Jonathan and buried the bones under a tamarisk tree. David loved these men for keeping the bodies of Saul and Jonathan from any more humiliation.

David sent these brave men a message, "The Lord bless you for showing this kindness to your King Saul."

---

*2 Samuel 1:23
†2 Samuel 1:26

David learned that Abner, Saul's cousin, had survived the battle. Abner had hurriedly declared Ish-Bosheth, one of Saul's surviving sons, the new king. Representatives of Ish-Bosheth and David, including Abner and David's nephew Joab, met in Gibeon to discuss peace. A vicious fight broke out among several hundred soldiers. Abner killed Asahel, Joab's brother. Naturally Joab tried to kill Abner.

"Must our swords devour each other forever?" cried Abner. "Must Jews kill Jews?"

Joab learned that Abner had not started the fight. In fact, he had defended himself against Asahel only after pleading with him several times to stop. So the men put down their arms. Many soldiers had been killed in the fight, and nothing had been accomplished. Joab took his men back to Hebron.

A truce of sorts was maintained, but over the years David grew stronger, and the successor to King Saul grew weaker. David's own family grew strong. He had taken four more wives: Maacah, Haggith, Abital, and Eglah. Ahinoam bore Amnon, David's first son; Abigail had his second son, Kileab; Maacah had his son Absalom; Haggith had a son named Adonijah; Abital had a son named Shephatiah; and Eglah had a son named Ithream. So in Hebron, David had six wives and six sons.

In the meantime, Ish-Bosheth had quarreled with Abner. So Abner negotiated with David to make David king of all the Jews. But Joab did not trust Abner and urged David to arrest Abner. David refused. He was very angry later when he learned that Joab waylaid Abner and killed him. Joab had waited years to avenge his brother Asahel's death. Even though Joab was his nephew, David was furious at his treachery. He wept at Abner's tomb at Hebron. He sang a song in his honor:

Should Abner have died as the lawless die?
Your hands were not bound,
your feet were not fettered.
You fell as one falls before wicked men.*

The people wept, too, and realized David had nothing to do with Abner's murder. When Ish-Bosheth heard of Abner's death, he was very frightened. His general Abner had been his main supporter. With Abner gone, Ish-Bosheth's followers might turn on him. That was exactly what happened. Two brothers named Recab and Baanah killed Ish-Bosheth. They brought his head all the way to Hebron to show David. But they had badly misjudged David. He ordered their execution.

With Ish-Bosheth dead, all the Jewish tribes rallied around David. At thirty-seven years of age, David was finally king of all the Jews. The Philistines heard of this, too. They knew David well and decided they must crush him before he became any stronger. David learned they had sent an army after him. He and his own army beat the Philistines while

---

*2 Samuel 3:33–34

they were camped at the Valley of Rephaim.

But the Philistines were not to be deterred by one defeat. They marched on David again. This time David let the Philistines attack. He commanded his troops to circle the enemy's army and attack them from behind. Once again the Philistines were beaten.

Then David went on the attack and drove the Philistines out of the Jewish highlands. He no longer commanded just six hundred men or one thousand. His army had thirty thousand men. They were well disciplined. His armies even defeated the Philistines on their own coastal plain where they were supposedly unbeatable. He smashed them back right up to the walls of their largest cities.

"It is not my strength but God's strength that powers the Jewish army!" he cried.

Never had the Jews been so mighty. The Philistines were thoroughly beaten. David then revealed his plans for the reunited Israel.

CHAPTER 6

To begin his plan, King David wanted Jerusalem to become the main city of his new Israel. But first, David's Jewish armies had to do the impossible. They had to conquer Jerusalem. The city was bordered on the west, the south, and the east by deep valleys. Invading armies couldn't make it up the steep sides of the valleys without first being driven away.

The north side of Jerusalem had been fortified by a huge number of trenches and other obstacles. Even the Philistines had never forced their way into Jerusalem. How could David conquer this mighty fortress?

"Jerusalem has always been able to withstand any long siege because it somehow has a supply of water," he told his army commanders.

Jerusalem was only a few miles from where David had shepherded flocks for many years. He knew natural springs of water could occur in very obscure places. Many springs were known only to a handful of people. He thought Jerusalem must have a spring like that.

"Suppose the spring is not within the city itself?" he asked.

"But that seems unlikely," objected one of his commanders.

"Perhaps. But I command you to send scouts all around the base of the walls of the city."

"But they hurl stones down on people who snoop around the walls."

"Do it at night."

During this nighttime prowling, one scout found a spring below the base of the eastern wall of the city. David insisted his scout explore the spring until he knew exactly where the water went. It was that further effort that revealed the spring water was entering a tunnel that ran below the east wall of the city. David's commanders eagerly planned to block the tunnel.

David prayed a long while about the plan and then told his commanders not to do it. Instead, some men must enter the tunnel and follow the path of the water. It was to his honor that many men offered to carry out this very scary task.

"It runs into a large pool below the city," explained his volunteers when they returned. "Their women lower water buckets with ropes down a shaft to gather water from the pool."

"Women do not retrieve water at night," said David. "That's when we will strike. We have all night to run a ladder up the shaft."

"Let us enter our very strongest soldiers!" said Joab eagerly. "I will gladly lead hundreds of soldiers through the tunnel and up the shaft into the heart of the city. We will have the northern gates open to the rest of our army before the people of Jerusalem discover what is happening!"

So the first moonless night, Joab led his best warriors into the water tunnel. With men that brave and that determined, the conquest of Jerusalem was simple and swift. Jerusalem became King David's city, the City of David! David terraced his new city and built a great palace out of cedars from Lebanon. He demanded that his first wife, Michal, be returned to him.

Then David had the Ark of the Covenant brought to Jerusalem. Never had he felt such joy. Wearing his ephod, he danced wildly around the procession bringing the ark. Musicians filled the streets. Joy sounded from cymbals, trumpets, flutes, harps, lyres, tambourines, sistrums, and lutes.

The ark was placed in the Most Holy Place—the room of the tabernacle that David had set up according to the strict Law of Moses. Sacrifices were made to God. David also had a feast that treated everyone in Jerusalem. At the end of a wonderful day, he found only one person in the city unhappy.

"How vulgar to dance around the ark like all those silly women did!" hissed Michal.

"I celebrated for the Lord. Only you feel humiliated by it," David said. At that moment, David knew Michal no longer loved him.

David was sad about Michal's coldness, but he forged ahead with his plans. He called his main prophet, who was now Nathan. David asked Nathan if it was wrong for him to live in a great cedar palace while the Ark of the Covenant—the very seat of Almighty God—resided in a tabernacle of animal hides. He asked Nathan if there was any reason why he shouldn't build God a great temple of cedar or stone.

That night, God told Nathan to give David a message. The next day, Nathan told the king that God did not want him to build a temple of cedar or stone. David's job was to unite the Jews into a great nation. Nathan said God would give one of David's descendants the job of building the temple.

David realized how greatly God had blessed him and his descendants. "How great you are, O Sovereign LORD! There is no one like you, and there is no God but you."*

Music was part of Jewish services, but David used it more than it had been used in the past. Several priests of the tribe of Levi helped him build a choir of several thousand singers and musicians. The musicians played harps, lutes, and cymbals to songs, called psalms, suitable for chanting in the worship of God. David had written dozens of psalms himself. Every emotion, every thought was conveyed to God. His psalms asked for God's help, praised God, showed sorrow, and celebrated how great God was.

In the years ahead, David found Jonathan's only living descendant, a crippled young man named Mephibosheth. David took him into his palace and treated him like one of his own sons. David's family was very large.

His armies conquered more neighboring nations, including the Moabites and the Arameans. His armies fought Zobah, Hamath, the Amalekites, the Edomites, and the Ammonites.

---

*2 Samuel 7:22

His army ventured far north to subdue the Syrians.

After ten years in Jerusalem, it seemed to David that he had everything. Then one spring evening, he looked down over the city from his palace roof and saw a woman bathing. She was so beautiful he was overcome with desire for her. He wanted her for his wife. He sent a servant to find out who she was.

"She is Bathsheba, the wife of Uriah," said the servant when he returned.

"Bathsheba," murmured David.

Although he was forty-seven years old and had many wives, David could scarcely think straight because he was so taken with this woman. He had come to expect his every wish to be satisfied. He summoned Bathsheba. When he met her, he was smitten by her beauty.

David decided he was going to marry Bathsheba. David knew Uriah was an officer in his army. In fact, Uriah was with Joab, who was currently leading the fighting against the Ammonites at their main city of Rabbah. Rabbah was about twenty miles east of the River Jordan. Located on the heavily traveled trade route called the King's Highway, Rabbah was considered quite a prize. David was intensely interested in the outcome of the fighting. But now he schemed against his own officer: Uriah!

David sent a message to Joab:

"Put Uriah in the front line where the fighting is

*fiercest. Then withdraw from him so he will be
struck down and die."*

Then David sat back and waited. Several days later, a
messenger arrived from the front lines.

---

*2 Samuel 11:15

CHAPTER 7

The messenger from Rabbah stood at attention before David. "Ammonites came out against us from the city gate—"

"Yes, yes, go on!" David sputtered impatiently.

"But we drove them back—"

"Yes, go on!"

"Then archers shot arrows at us—"

"Go on!"

"Some of your men died—"

David rose menacingly. "Finish your report!"

"Moreover, your servant Uriah is dead."

David could barely keep from rejoicing. "Tell Joab that these losses must not upset him. One man dies in battle as well as another. Press the attack. Destroy Rabbah!"

When the messenger departed, David collapsed in his throne. The deed was done. Bathsheba was his. All that separated her from David was her period of mourning for her dead husband. Then David would bring her into the palace as his wife!

From the palace, he observed people rushing into Bathsheba's house. Soon loud wailing was heard. Because Uriah was wealthy, his family hired additional mourners to wail and chant their grief. Even musicians were hired to play heartrending dirges on their flutes. All the while David waited impatiently in the palace.

Even when Joab and David's army returned in triumph after leaving Rabbah in ruins, David was distracted by his wait. Finally, after several weeks, Bathsheba was brought into the palace. David and Bathsheba loved each other very much.

One day Nathan, David's main prophet, asked for an audience. David agreed, somewhat surprised that Nathan insisted they meet privately. Nathan told him a story:

"There were two men in a certain town, one rich and the other poor. The rich man had a very large number of sheep and cattle, but the poor man had nothing except one little ewe lamb he had bought. He raised it, and it grew up with him and his children. It shared his food, drank from his cup and even slept in his arms. It was like a daughter to him.

"Now a traveler came to the rich man, but the rich man refrained from taking one of his own sheep or cattle to prepare a meal for the traveler who had come to him. Instead, he took the ewe lamb that belonged to the poor man and prepared it for the one who had come to him."*

David exploded in anger. "What? As surely as Almighty God is alive that rich man should die!"

---

*2 Samuel 12:1–4

Nathan looked David straight in the eye. "You, Sir, are that rich man."

"Me?"

"You have many wives, yet you took the one wife of Uriah by having him killed by the sword of the Ammonites. For that great sin, your family will endure disaster after disaster."

David retreated to a private room, reeling. What had he done? By his sin he had brought God's wrath against his own family! Always the poet, he composed a song of sorrow which started with a confession:

> *Have mercy on me, O God,*
> *according to your unfailing love;*
> *according to your great compassion*
> *blot out my transgressions.*
> *Wash away all my iniquity*
> *and cleanse me from my sin.*
>
> *For I know my transgressions,*
> *and my sin is always before me.**

Near the end of his sad song, David begged for forgiveness:

> *Create in me a pure heart, O God,*
> *and renew a steadfast spirit within me.*

---

*Psalm 51:1–3

Do not cast me from your presence
or take your Holy Spirit from me.
Restore to me the joy of your salvation
and grant me a willing spirit, to sustain me.

Then I will teach transgressors your ways,
and sinners will turn back to you.
Save me from bloodguilt, O God,
the God who saves me, and my tongue
*will sing of your righteousness.**

David had confessed his sin. He had repented. But that did not relieve him of God's punishment. The first disaster soon struck. Bathsheba gave birth to a son, but the baby got sick. David pleaded with God to let the boy live.

The baby died.

"I will go to him, but he will not return to me," David said sadly about his dead son.

David meant that he would join his son in eternity. David loved God, and God loved him in spite of his sinfulness. A song one of his priests had composed expressed his feeling:

But God will redeem my life from the grave;
he will surely take me to himself.†

---

*Psalm 51:10–14
†Psalm 49:15

But David had little time to mourn. Never had his kingdom made so many demands on him. His inner circle included Ahithophel and Hushai, his counselors; Jehoshaphat and Sheva, his recorders; Nathan, his prophet; and Abiathar and Jairite, his personal priests.

Constantly he agonized over who to assign to which jobs. Of course Joab, his highest general, ran his large royal army, but David approved of every assignment, every promotion. Hashabiah and Zadok administered a very complex organization of priests and musicians in the tabernacle. Each of the twelve Jewish tribes also had to have a leader who was loyal to the king. David assigned his own tribe of Judah to his brother Elihu and gave the tribe of Simeon to his son Shephatiah.

The royal property required much oversight because David was now the wealthiest of the wealthy. He had faithful managers in charge of the storehouses, the field workers, the vineyards, the orchards, the olive presses, the stables of donkeys and camels, and the vast herds of cattle, sheep, and goats. But because of Nathan's warning, David worried over what disaster would next strike his family.

He soon found out.

Amnon, David and Ahinoam's son, was a young man. One day Amnon pretended to be sick. He stayed in his bedroom and asked David to send Tamar to visit him. She was such a comforting person.

Tamar was Amnon's half-sister. She was the daughter of

David and Maacah. So David sent Tamar to visit Amnon.

Later, Tamar's brother Absalom saw her. He was shocked. Tamar's eyes were red from weeping. She had put ashes on her head and torn her elegant robe.

"What has happened?" gasped Absalom. "Did Amnon attack you?"

Tears poured down Tamar's face.

"Don't worry, my sister," Absalom said. "Come live in my house. I will protect you."

When David learned what had happened, he was very angry. But he did not punish Amnon for attacking his sister. This made Absalom very angry. He loved his sister and thought Amnon should pay for attacking her. He waited for a chance to get even with Amnon.

Two years later, all of David's sons went to the annual sheep shearing in late spring. Absalom was in charge. David had thousands of sheep, and when the shearing was finished the workers celebrated. But the news David got from the shearing was not joyous. While all the sons were enjoying the party, Absalom had his servants kill Amnon!

"It was because Amnon attacked his sister Tamar," said David's nephew Jonadab.

Absalom was glad that he had paid back Amnon for what he had done. But Absalom was afraid that he would now be punished. So Absalom ran away to the nation of Geshur, located east of the Sea of Galilee. Geshur welcomed him because his mother, Maacah, was the daughter of one of its kings.

David mourned the loss of both of his sons. Amnon was dead, and Absalom might as well have been dead. He was living far away, and David could not forgive him. It was three years before Joab, David's nephew and head general, persuaded David to let Absalom return to the palace.

"After all, didn't Amnon attack Absalom's sister Tamar?" Joab reminded the king. "Because of that attack, Tamar has never married or had children."

"Go get him then," agreed David. "But I won't see him."

So Absalom returned. Most people did not blame him for his crime. Besides, Absalom was one of the most handsome men in the kingdom. His glossy black hair was full and long like the magnificent mane of a lion. Of all the Jews, only Absalom drove a chariot attended by fifty footmen. The people were thrilled with his flair for the colorful. After Absalom had been back in Jerusalem for two years, David finally forgave him.

But rumors soon reached David that Absalom was endearing himself to all the visiting dignitaries by entertaining them and promising them favors with the king. There was no doubt that Absalom was popular—but at what price? And what was he planning to do with that popularity?

Several years later, Absalom told David, "I wish to go to Hebron and worship God."

"Go in peace," said David.

David was now nearly sixty years old. He thought that Absalom's trip was unusual because the young man was not known for loving God and going to services. Moreover, Absalom had invited two hundred of the most important Jews in Israel to go with him. Later, David learned his chief counselor, Ahithophel, was also at Hebron. Yes, the gathering seemed most unusual.

One day a soldier burst in. "I come from Hebron. Absalom has declared himself king of all the Jews!"

David quickly assessed his situation. Absalom had engineered a very successful rebellion. Although Joab remained faithful to David, most of the army was under Absalom's control. No doubt he was marching on Jerusalem that very moment.

"We must flee Jerusalem!" David heard himself saying.

Imagine, after ruling for so many years, he was fleeing his own City of David! He still possessed an army of several thousand soldiers including his royal guard. But he would not be trapped within the city and have his loyal followers starved by Absalom. Besides, David was the master of surviving in the wilderness.

With his army and his household, he marched down from his great walled city into the Kidron Valley east of Jerusalem. Then David's party marched up the Mount of Olives with its rich orchards. There, David told the priests Zadok and Abiathar that they must go back to Jerusalem and remain at the tabernacle to protect the Ark of the Covenant.

Then David instructed his loyal counselor Hushai, "You must go back, too. Pledge your allegiance to Absalom. But foil his plans any way you can. And send information to me in the wilderness through the two sons of Zadok and Abiathar. I will await them at the River Jordan."

With those final instructions, David and his followers marched off into the wilderness. At first, they traveled the well-used road to Jericho. Few roads were steeper. The travelers left Jerusalem in the cool highlands and descended to Jericho in the blistering lowlands. On the way, David's entourage passed a man named Shimei. Shimei was one of the few survivors of the house of King Saul.

"Curse you, King David!" screamed Shimei. "God has repaid you for all the blood on your hands!"

Abishai, Joab's brother and David's nephew, growled, "Let me go kill that dog."

"Leave him alone," snapped David. "If my own son Absalom is trying to kill me, why are you concerned with this relative of King Saul?"

Then David led his party off the main road and down a ravine to the River Jordan. There they waited for the two sons of the priests to come. Days passed before the two young men showed up. Breathlessly, they told David that Absalom wanted to set out for David immediately but that Hushai had advised him to build a huge force first. Now David had time to cross the River Jordan and hide in the eastern mountains.

CHAPTER 8

So David crossed the River Jordan and marched on to the Ammonite city of Mahanaim. Although David had long fought the Ammonites, they respected him. He was welcome. The tired travelers were furnished bedding and utensils. They ate heartily of bread, beans, lentils, cheese, and honey.

"We must prepare to battle Absalom's army," David said to Joab and two other commanders. "We will divide the forces into three groups. I will march with you."

"No!" objected Joab. "You are worth ten thousand of us. If Absalom's troops recognize you, they will never stop until they kill you."

"I won't go then, but please spare my son Absalom," he pleaded.

So David waited in the city, getting reports of armies moving here and there. Soon it became clear that Joab—a great general—had lured Absalom's army into the forests north of Mahanaim. Absalom's superior numbers did him no good at all. His men scattered through the forest, lost and bewildered. Joab's more disciplined troops cut them down. Many deserted Absalom's army.

David waited within the walls of Mahanaim. Soon he learned that Absalom's army had been routed. But what of

Absalom? He was killed.

David screamed, "Oh my son Absalom! My son, my son Absalom! If only I had died instead of you!"

David felt enormous guilt over Absalom. If he had handled the situation with Tamar the way a father should have, Absalom would not have been tempted to commit murder and go into exile. Then David had ignored his son for many years. Who knew how bitter the experience had made Absalom?

The details of Absalom's death depressed David even more. Absalom's long, flowing hair had gotten tangled in a tree. Helpless, he had been speared many times by David's army. Joab threw the first spear.

David railed, "Didn't I tell Joab and his army not to kill Absalom?"

But Joab was just as angry. He went to talk to King David. "It seems you love those who hate you and hate those who love you," he said. "You would be pleased if Absalom were alive today and all of us were dead!"

Although David was sick at heart and wanted to kill Joab, he didn't. Joab was right in being angry with him. Joab and his other loyal followers had saved his kingdom. Besides, David felt his own sin had created problems for Absalom. Nathan had warned David long ago that God would forgive him but that David would still be punished.

Still, David returned to Jerusalem in triumph. But age slowed him more and more. Once, perhaps feeling guilty because he sat out the great battle in the forests north of Mahanaim, David joined a skirmish with the Philistines to the west. During the battle the weight of his armor made him so tired that he collapsed. His nephew Abishai struck down one of the giants of Gath just as he bore down on David.

"Never again!" swore David's commanders. They tried to soften their anger by saying, "We will not let the lamp of Israel be extinguished."

David's commanders were right. He must rule. For his ability to run the kingdom remained strong. So did his creative ability as Israel's singer of songs. David still composed psalms:

The LORD is my rock, my fortress and my deliverer; my God is my rock, in whom I take refuge. He is my shield and the horn of my salvation, my stronghold. I call to the LORD, who is worthy of praise, and I am saved from my enemies. *

David wrote down the names of his greatest warriors, whom he called his mighty men. Among the thirty-seven men listed was Uriah. How terrible David felt as he wrote that name. He had murdered one of his own mighty men! He shuddered. But it seemed as he approached seventy years of age that he could not stop shuddering. Would he be able to

---

*Psalm 18:2–3

control another rebellious son? He soon found out.

This time it was Adonijah, David and Haggith's son, who plotted to become king. He was pulling people away from David, including Joab and Abiathar. Perhaps these two loyal followers felt David was now too feeble to govern. Would Adonijah succeed at what Absalom had failed to do?

But Bathsheba knew what few people knew. "Did you not swear to me," she asked David, "that our son Solomon would inherit your throne?"

"That was commanded not by me but by God," answered David. "My prophet Nathan told me." David also knew that Solomon would build the great temple of stone that God would not allow him to build.

At that moment Nathan angrily entered. "Have you told Adonijah he is to inherit the throne? He is celebrating already."

David had reigned for forty years. He realized he could no longer cling to the throne. He gave his last commands: "Have Zadok the high priest anoint Solomon king of Israel immediately. Blow the trumpets and shout, 'Long live King Solomon!' "

With the announcement that twenty-one-year-old Solomon was king, there was great jubilation. Adonijah's ambition evaporated. His allies deserted him. But Solomon spared his brother's life after warning him to go home and cause no trouble. Knowing Adonijah as he did, David doubted the man could keep out of trouble.

At seventy, David's health failed rapidly. He was an old ram, but God would shepherd him to the end. He sang one of his songs that said exactly what was in his heart and soul:

The LORD is my shepherd, I shall not be in want.
He makes me lie down in green pastures, he leads
me beside quiet waters, he restores my soul.
He guides me in paths of righteousness for his
name's sake.
Even though I walk through the valley of the shadow
of death,
I will fear no evil, for you are with me; your rod and
your staff, they comfort me.
You prepare a table before me in the presence of my
enemies.
You anoint my head with oil; my cup overflows.
Surely goodness and love will follow me all the days
of my life, and I will dwell in the house of the
LORD forever.*

"I am about to go the way of all flesh," David told Solomon. "Be strong, show yourself a man, and obey God. Walk in His ways, and keep His commandments as written in the Law of Moses. Some day one of our descendants will

---

*Psalm 23

be Messiah of Israel."

One thousand years later, one of David's descendants was born in Bethlehem. He was Jesus of Nazareth, the Messiah, the Son of God.

DANIEL

EVER-FAITHFUL PROPHET

by Ellen Caughey

CHAPTER 1

The temperature outside the massive stone palace of King Nebuchadnezzar must have been at least 110 degrees—but inside you could hear teeth chattering and knees rattling. After bowing nervously in front of the throne, the king's magicians now stood as if they were freezing cold. In truth, they were scared to death.

King Nebuchadnezzar, ruler of the empire of Babylon, had just awakened from a very troubling sleep. "I have had a dream that troubles me, and I want to know what it means," he declared from his mighty perch.

In a sweeping movement, Aliabad, the chief magician (or astrologer, as he was known), bowed once again before the king. "O King, live forever!" he cried, giving the standard greeting to the king. "Tell your servants the dream, and we will interpret it."

Stroking his mangled beard, Aliabad tried to look like he knew what he was doing. He and his fellow astrologers had succeeded in pleasing the king in the past. But just about anyone could flatter the king with a phony horoscope or fine fortune. Aliabad had a feeling this time was different.

All eyes were glued on Nebuchadnezzar.

"Oh, you astrologers who think you know everything! This is what I have decided: If you do not tell me what my dream was and what it means, I will have you cut into pieces!" The king's voice echoed throughout the palace chamber.

The astrologers had never heard such a request! How were they to know what the king had dreamed? As they gathered together several yards from the throne, their hands were moving up and down, their eyes were rolling, their heads were shaking in unison, and their wild whispers sounded like a beehive just discovered by a bear.

King Nebuchadnezzar flashed the trembling astrologers a wicked grin. "Don't think I don't know what you're doing—you're trying to buy time! So let me tell you again, in case you didn't hear right the first time. If you tell me the dream, I will know you can tell me what it means. If not. . ." Closing his eyes, the king plopped a giant fig into his mouth.

Once again a shaking Aliabad threw himself on the floor, his robes flying behind him. "There is not a man on earth who can do what the king asks! No one can tell the king what he dreamed—except maybe the gods, who do not live with us." (Aliabad was speaking of gods that men had created to explain the changes in weather and the seasons, and why good and bad things happen to people.)

At that, the king's face turned deep red, and he rose from his chair, flinging the fig stem onto the ground. "How dare you," he began slowly, his anger rising. "Today every one of you will die!" Then, turning to a servant who was trying to look invisible, he added, "And while you're at it, find Daniel and his friends. Put them all to death!"

The swooshing sound of his silk robes as the king strode out could not compete with the terrified cries of Aliabad and the others.

CHAPTER 2

Daniel and his three friends, Hananiah, Mishael, and Azariah, were well known throughout the palace of King Nebuchadnezzar. Just three years before, in 605 B.C. (more than six hundred years before the birth of Jesus), the four of them had been brought to Babylon from Jerusalem in the land of Judah. Because Nebuchadnezzar (and his armies) had conquered Judah, he had the right to bring back to his country whatever Jews he wanted to be slaves.

But the king was a wise ruler, and he wanted to remain one for years to come. So he selected certain young men of Judah—handsome, well educated, and from noble families —for special training. One day, after years of learning to speak the Babylonian language and to read ancient books, especially those on mathematics and astrology, these men would give the king advice on important matters, like predicting the future or interpreting dreams.

Twelve-year-old Daniel and his friends were among those chosen and then carted away—five hundred miles to the east of Jerusalem—to the luxurious palace of the great Nebuchadnezzar in the city of Babylon.

From Jerusalem, the caravans of Nebuchadnezzar headed north, across the rugged mountains of Syria and Aram to reach the bustling city of Aleppo. The course was then set to the east, finally encountering the great Euphrates River at the city of Tiphsah.

And from Tiphsah, the captives from Judah followed the river's southeast path for many months until they finally reached the city of Babylon, the capital of the Babylonian empire.

As the four friends passed under the Ishtar Gate, the main entrance into the city, they couldn't help staring up. "Have you ever seen a city like this?" Daniel asked.

Mishael couldn't help noticing the lions and dragons created by the yellow and brown colors of brick that decorated the Ishtar Gate. From a distance, the gate had seemed to be made entirely of purple. "Are there really dragons and lions in Babylon?"

Daniel made a funny face at his friend. "Oh, Mishael. Did the rabbis not tell you about all the strange gods they worship here? I think the dragon is the symbol of their god Marduk—"

Hananiah interrupted. "And the lion stands for the goddess Ishtar, is that correct?"

Azariah summed up their situation perfectly. "Well, we are not in Judah anymore. That's for sure!"

On their first complete morning in the palace, the four friends found themselves seated on colorful, overstuffed pillows, trying to memorize the Chaldean alphabet, the one used by all Babylonians. But that wasn't all they were having trouble getting used to. Upon entering the king's service, they had each been given a new Babylonian name.

Daniel would now be called Belteshazzar, after the Babylonian god Bel; Hananiah would be known as Shadrach, or one "inspired by the sun-god"; Mishael was now called Meshach, which meant "who is comparable to Shak," another name for the goddess Venus; and Azariah would forever be addressed as Abednego, or a "servant of the fire god."

Tall for his age, Daniel stretched his long arms over his head and gave a frustrated yell. "I have had it! Who among us likes these names?"

Silence.

Then Hananiah had an idea. "Let's use our old names when we're together. When we're with the king, well, I will have to get used to being a sun god."

Azariah's eyes opened wide. "Does that mean I will be able to breathe fire out of my mouth?"

Daniel leaned over and punched his arm in response. "Let's be serious for a minute. Just in case we forget what our old names mean, I'm going to write them somewhere, in our old language. We may be here awhile."

On separate lines on a small piece of papyrus, Daniel wrote the following:

Daniel, "God is my judge."

Hananiah, "whom God hath favored."

Mishael, "who is comparable to God?"

Azariah, "whom God helps."

Daniel then motioned for the four of them to stand. He

read aloud what he had written on the papyrus. Then he tucked the crinkled scrap inside his belt. "Today, right now, let us make a promise before God. No matter what happens to us here in Babylon, no matter if we never see our families in Jerusalem again, no matter what—we will serve the one and only God, the Most High God, El Elyon."

As the four friends put their hands together, Daniel said, "As long as God is on our side, we will not be afraid."

Just then, loud footsteps came to a halt outside their room, and Ashpenaz, the chief of King Nebuchadnezzar's court officials, entered grandly.

"Uhh-umm! Begging your pardon, young sirs, but lunch is served!"

Barely visible under the weight of the enormous golden tray was Ashpenaz's young assistant, Melzar, who managed to set his burden down without too much difficulty. There on the king's tray was more food than Daniel, Mishael, Hananiah, and Azariah had ever seen—tall urns filled with wine, fruits and nuts of all kinds, figs and olives, and sticky looking cakes dripping with honey. But what caught the boys' attention was the head of a pig surrounded by thick, juicy slices of pork and lamb!

"Well?" Ashpenaz broke the silence. "The king himself has requested that you eat what he eats. Such an honor for such young men!"

"I am afraid we cannot eat anything on this tray," Daniel said, his eyes meeting Melzar's for a minute before facing

Ashpenaz. "It is not that we don't appreciate everything the king is doing for us, but—"

Ashpenaz interrupted him immediately. "But what?" His bushy black eyebrows seemed to meet in the middle of his wrinkled forehead.

Smothering his grin, Daniel thought he was looking at one very active, furry caterpillar. "You see, as Jews, my friends and I must not eat this food. If we take one bite, we will be going against everything our parents taught us, and everything God wants us to do."

The laws of the Jews, given to Moses from God, were very specific about what foods, and what animals, could and could not be eaten.

Azariah nodded his head. "Take that pig—no Jew can eat that!"

Mishael, Hananiah, and Daniel were almost laughing at the thought of what their mothers would do to them if they even considered such a meal.

The boys couldn't explain to Ashpenaz and Melzar every reason why the king's food was unacceptable. But any grown-up Jewish person would have known that the first serving of Nebuchadnezzar's food was offered to idols, not to the one true God. And the first portion of wine was poured out on an altar used to worship these idols.

Ashpenaz was silent for a moment. He seemed to be considering what the boys said. "King Nebuchadnezzar, long may he reign, has given you this food, and you reject it all!

You know, you aren't the only boys the king is preparing to be his advisers. What if the king sees you and thinks you don't look so good? And then he finds out you aren't eating his food? What do you think the great King Nebuchadnezzar will do to me?"

Like the goblets on the golden tray that rattled back and forth, Daniel and his three friends seemed a little nervous. But not one made a move toward the tray.

"Lizard got your tongues or, should I say, your stomachs? My fine friends, should you refuse the king's food, my head—and not that pig's—might be on that tray!"

At that the four boys cried out together, "No, no, no!"

Daniel then stood and faced Ashpenaz and Melzar. He took a deep breath and tried to appear older than his twelve years. "Please, I have an idea. Give us nothing to eat but vegetables and nothing to drink but water for ten days. Then compare how we look with the other boys who have eaten the king's food."

Ashpenaz and Melzar paced the length of the oriental carpet, their heads bowed, their voices muffled. Finally, Melzar spoke. "Ten days only, Belteshazzar, then we shall see."

For ten days, Daniel, Mishael, Hananiah, and Azariah drank only water and ate only vegetables, while the other young men in the king's training feasted on rich and exotic foods. And they prayed three times a day, as was their custom, facing west in the direction of Jerusalem. They prayed that God would give them strength.

Now the moment had arrived. Who would look healthier?

When Daniel and his friends joined the others in the courtyard of the palace, Ashpenaz and Melzar peered carefully at the group. Then Melzar whispered in Ashpenaz's ear, and the older man smiled knowingly.

"Water and vegetables for everyone!"

Daniel, Mishael, Hananiah, and Azariah looked so much better than the other boys that now everyone would eat the way they did—by order of the king. That night as he said his prayers, Daniel thanked God for giving him the courage to take a stand for his faith. God had led him to this strange country, to this magnificent palace, and to this curious king for a reason.

CHAPTER 3

The determined footsteps of King Nebuchadnezzar's chief officer echoed down the stone hallways of the palace fortress. But Arioch, a towering, muscular soldier, was not at all eager to do what the king had ordered. While other guards had been sent to find Daniel and his three friends, he alone had been ordered to put the astrologers to death. They were a slimy bunch, those magicians, and Arioch could imagine what crazy things they would say to him: "A curse on your family dog!" "May your skin turn green and your hair fall out!"

Then Arioch thought about Daniel. Somehow, no matter what Arioch said to Daniel, Daniel had a way of answering him that made everything seem all right. The word around the palace was that Daniel, Mishael, Hananiah, and Azariah had ten times the wisdom of the other young men in training—not to mention the astrologers!—and something more. The word around the palace was that some god was on their side, the one Daniel simply called God.

Shaking his head, Arioch thought to himself how Daniel would need his God now—more than ever. And then Arioch saw him, turning the corner just ahead, his face almost covered up by the book he was reading.

"Daniel! Just the person I wanted to see," Arioch boomed

out, voicing a lie.

"Arioch, I didn't see you coming," Daniel apologized.

Arioch breathed a huge sigh.

"Something is wrong, terribly wrong, isn't it?" As usual, Daniel knew what to say.

"Yes, my young friend. I may as well tell you." So Arioch retold in great detail the troubled sleep of the king and the king's strange request of the astrologers. Finally, the king's chief officer revealed what the king had in mind for Daniel and his friends.

But Daniel did not look worried. "Why did the king order all of us to die?" he asked calmly.

Arioch tried to explain, but he could see Daniel was already forming a plan.

"I must see the king right away!" Daniel announced, then turned, almost running toward the king's chambers. Arioch raised his hand to stop him, but it was too late.

An hour later, Daniel was seen leaving the king's chambers to find Hananiah, Mishael, and Azariah. He was alive and well, but in a hurry. What had happened between Daniel and the king?

Piecing together bits of information, Arioch was able to tell the story. "I can't believe he said this but he did," he told a group of fellow guards later over dinner. "Unlike those silly magicians who said they could only tell what the dream means, Daniel is going to do the impossible, my friends. He saved his life and the lives of his friends by asking for time—

to tell the king the dream and what it means. I only hope he knows what he's doing!"

Candles flickered around the darkened room as Hananiah, Mishael, and Azariah listened closely to Daniel. "We have only one answer. We must ask God to tell us the mystery of King Nebuchadnezzar's dream. Only God knows what the king dreamed."

For the next several hours, the friends prayed and prayed, often lying facedown on the cold stone floor. Sometimes they cried out loud, and sometimes only soft whispers could be heard. Then Daniel opened his eyes.

"Praise be the name of God forever and ever!" he shouted. "Wisdom and power are His! He reveals deep and hidden things! I thank and praise You, the God of my fathers—"

"Daniel, Daniel, did God speak to you? What did He say?" Hananiah asked eagerly.

"My friends, I must see Arioch at the first light. God has made known to me the dream of the king."

Arioch was smiling broadly when he greeted Daniel outside his room. "So, you can do what the king has ordered?"

But Daniel did not return his smile. "Do not kill the astrologers, Arioch. Take me to the king."

As they approached King Nebuchadnezzar's throne, the king's eyes were closed as if he were asleep. But then his arm shot up, causing Daniel and Arioch to freeze in their steps. "Well?" the king's voice boomed. "Are you able to tell me what I saw in my dream and what it means?" One eye opened and fastened on Daniel.

"Not I, King Nebuchadnezzar, but God has revealed the mystery of your dream!"

Daniel swallowed, then continued. "God has shown King Nebuchadnezzar what will happen in days to come. I do not possess greater wisdom than others; I am only being used by God so that you will understand your dream."

The king nodded, and a slow smile crept across his face.

Daniel cleared his throat. "In your dream you saw before you a large statue, an enormous, awesome statue! The head was made of pure gold, its chest and arms were silver, and its stomach and thighs were made from bronze. The legs of the statue were iron, but the feet and ten toes were made partly of iron and partly of baked clay."

The king's smile quickly faded. As he gulped the wine from his massive silver goblet, he motioned Daniel with a flick of his hand. "Go on, go on."

"Suddenly, from out of nowhere, a rock not cut by human hands appeared and smashed the statue, breaking it to pieces! And then the wind swept the pieces away."

Daniel paused a moment, then continued. "But the rock that came from nowhere became a huge mountain and filled the whole earth. This was your dream."

The king nodded again, his eyes fixed on Daniel. "Yes, that was my dream. But what does it mean? Did your God tell you that, too?"

"The head of gold is you, King Nebuchadnezzar. The

God of heaven has given you power over men and women, animals and birds. He has made you ruler over them all. But after you, other kingdoms will arise, kingdoms not nearly as grand as yours, even one made of iron that will conquer everything it desires. Finally, the toes of the statue, made of iron and baked clay, are ten kings who will rule on the earth many years from now. But this kingdom will be partly strong and partly weak. At that time, the God of heaven will set up a kingdom on earth that will never be destroyed or conquered by other peoples, a kingdom that will last forever. That kingdom is the rock not cut by human hands, a rock out of a mountain."

The king's chambers were so quiet even the flies refused to buzz. Looking the king squarely in the eyes, Daniel said, "The great God has shown the king what will take place in the future. The dream is true and the interpretation is trustworthy."

At that, King Nebuchadnezzar stood and ran toward Daniel, falling on his face before him. Gasps could be heard all around—no one had ever seen a king as mighty as he worship another human being, especially a young man like Daniel!

"Surely your God is the God of gods and the Lord of kings!" Nebuchadnezzar cried. He then struggled to his feet. "Today I appoint you, Belteshazzar, ruler over the province of Babylon and ruler over all the astrologers of the palace."

"You are very generous, King Nebuchadnezzar," Daniel

answered. "I just have one favor to ask. . . ."

And on that same day, King Nebuchadnezzar appointed Hananiah, Mishael, and Azariah administrators over the province of Babylon. They would travel around the kingdom while Daniel remained at the palace.*

That night, Daniel could not sleep. Rising from his mat, he went up to the roof of the palace to gaze at the stars. And he was not disappointed. Against the inky blanket of night, delicately positioned, were what seemed like millions of precious diamonds. *And to think God knows the name of each star,* Daniel thought to himself.

"Why am I surprised?" he then asked no one in particular, for the guards were positioned a distance away from him. That day, God had performed an incredible miracle, one no man could do. That day, God had revealed himself to a powerful king, but a king who still believed God was one of many gods. "Why, God? Why?" he questioned the sky.

And then one answer came to him: God was not finished with the proud Nebuchadnezzar.

---

* Unlike those in the king's chambers in 602 B.C., you can tell which kingdoms represented what metals in King Nebuchadnezzar's dream. The silver chest and arms was the world empire of Medo-Persia, the bronze stomach and thighs represent Greece and the Macedonia of Alexander the Great, and the iron legs are the great Roman Empire that was in power when Jesus was born on earth. The feet and toes of iron and clay, or the ten kings, have yet to come into power but will do so before Jesus comes a second time. Someday Jesus will establish His perfect kingdom on earth—in other words, the rock not cut by human hands.

Even though many weeks had passed, King Nebuchadnezzar could not get his latest, most troubling dream out of his mind. And even though Daniel had interpreted the dream to his satisfaction, the king was still restless.

"You remember in my dream, Aliabad, how I was the head of gold?" King Nebuchadnezzar said to his astrologer one afternoon.

Nodding for the umpteenth time, Aliabad forced himself not to yawn. "Yes, O King, gold, more precious than all metals! And a kingdom of gold, grander than any empire!"

Stroking the first of his many chins, the king continued pacing his chamber. "My point exactly! But how will the world know? I must tell the world!"

Then, suddenly, the king collapsed on his throne and began laughing and clapping his hands. "I've got it, oh, this is so good! Why didn't I think of this before? But then, only I could have thought of such a lasting tribute, such a salute, such a statue!"

Aliabad turned his back on the king as if to cough, then rolled his eyes at the servants behind him. "Statue, did you say, King Nebuchadnezzar? Like that of a god?"

"Yes, yes, but so much better," said the king, sounding slightly displeased with Aliabad's limited thinking. "Picture this: a statue made entirely of gold, larger than any statue in Babylon! A statue set on a hill so that all peoples may know there is one Nebuchadnezzar, one Babylon—a statue that all peoples must bow down before and worship. Only in

Babylon can such a statue exist!"

"Only in Babylon" was not an exaggeration—at least not to the million or so Babylonians, and perhaps an even greater number outside Nebuchadnezzar's kingdom. For only in Babylon were there two of the seven wonders of the world, the magnificent "hanging gardens," and the amazing high wall that surrounded the city.

The gardens, which were built by Nebuchadnezzar to please his wife, Amytis, were not gardens at all, but a huge hill. This man-made hill rose to a height of three hundred fifty feet and had trees planted on either side of a ten-foot-wide staircase. Then there was the city wall, eighty-seven feet high and three hundred fifty feet wide—so wide that four chariots could ride side by side!

And now "only in Babylon" there would be a gleaming gold statue set high on the plain of Dura, a statue that would measure ninety feet tall and nine feet wide. A statue no one could miss!

A day of dedication was declared for King Nebuchadnezzar's statue, and all of Babylon gathered for the celebration. All the king's astrologers were there, led by Aliabad whose nose was held so high he nearly stumbled as he walked in the procession. Following them were the royal judges, governors, and treasurers.

And then there was King Nebuchadnezzar himself. Seated on a golden throne—"My favorite color!" he declared—the king then gave the signal to begin the ceremony.

"O people of Babylon," declared the king's herald (the one who makes royal announcements), "as soon as you hear the sound of the horn, flute, harp, and other instruments, you must fall down and worship the statue of gold. Those who do not will be thrown into a blazing furnace!"

Silence greeted the herald's terrifying pronouncement. This blazing furnace was really a huge industrial furnace used by Babylonian workers for baking bricks and smelting metals. Set outdoors, the furnace had a large opening at the top from which flames could be seen shooting up—hungry, devouring flames. To be thrown into the blazing furnace meant instant death.

And then the music began—beautiful melodies and grand, stirring chords—music fit to worship a king. And all the people fell down immediately and worshipped the golden statue of King Nebuchadnezzar.

All the people, that is, except Mishael, Hananiah, and Azariah.*

Lying on his stomach, Aliabad turned his head, and from the corner of his eye he could see them standing. His usual smile—kept in place for royal occasions—turned into a sneer. Poking another astrologer, he motioned to the three men who had refused to obey the king's command. "Look at them!" Aliabad hissed between his teeth. "Who do they think they are?"

---

* No record is given of Daniel's whereabouts that day. He may have been away from the city of Babylon on business for the king.

"But they—and Belteshazzar—saved our lives, Aliabad. We can't turn them in!"

"What you say is true. But I cannot just sit here and watch how they treat Nebuchadnezzar! The king has given them more riches than you could ever want. Maybe if we just call this little incident to the king's attention, he will reward us, his most loyal servants—don't you think?"

When the music ended, Aliabad eagerly struggled to his feet, hurriedly straightening his robes. First, he must inform the other astrologers of this act of disobedience and then. . .then he would lead them to the throne of King Nebuchadnezzar.

At last Meshach, Shadrach, and Abednego will know their rightful places in the king's palace, Aliabad thought to himself. *As ashes in his fireplace!*

After waiting for the crowds of people to bow one last time before the king, Aliabad had his opportunity. "What a day, King Nebuchadnezzar! And the golden statue and the music—why, not much could be better!"

"Not much, Aliabad? I thought my day was perfect! Was a musician out of tune?" The king was still smiling, but a look of concern had creased his forehead.

"No, no, nothing like that. I mean, it's not nothing, it's just. . ."

"SPEAK UP!" the king's voice thundered, and all eyes rested on Aliabad.

Aliabad came closer to the king, as if what he had to say was very private. "There are some Jews to whom you have given much power in Babylon, Jews who pay no attention to you, Jews who do not fall down and worship your statue!"

"Shadrach, Meshach, and Abednego? They did not worship the statue?" The king's voice was trembling with anger.

"I did not want to be the one to tell you, O King, but I felt someone should," Aliabad answered, managing not to smile.

"BRING THEM HERE AT ONCE!"

When they were brought before the throne, the three friends looked puzzled. His face almost purple with rage, the king was clearly upset with them.

"Is it true, Shadrach, Meshach, and Abednego, that you do not worship the statue of gold? That when you heard the music you did not fall down at once? IS THAT TRUE?" The king's finger pointed at them was shaking.

Shadrach, or Hananiah, spoke for the group. "O King, we serve only one God, the God of heaven, and He has commanded that we must not serve other gods. For that reason, we cannot worship the statue of gold."

"You tell me this, then. What god will be able to rescue you from the fiery furnace? Will yours?" Nebuchadnezzar glared fiercely at Shadrach.

"If we are thrown into the furnace, the God we serve is able to save us. But even if He does not, that is all right, too, because it is His will that we die."

"No, it is MY WILL that you die, and die today!" the king bellowed. Turning toward his nearest servant, the king ordered the furnace heated seven times hotter than usual.

And then he commanded that Shadrach, Meshach, and Abednego be thrown into the hungry flames.

Dressed in flowing robes and pants, with turbans covering their heads, Hananiah, Mishael, and Azariah were bound with ropes and led up a flight of steps to be thrown into the blazing furnace. But because King Nebuchadnezzar had ordered the furnace to be made hotter than usual, at the top of the steps, flames could be seen leaping several yards into the air. Anyone who came close would surely be burned to death.

And so it was that the servants who led the three men up the steps were killed instantly by the flames just as they threw the three men into the furnace.

Moments later, King Nebuchadnezzar went to a window built into the side of the furnace. His hand went to his mouth, and at first no words came out. "Weren't only three men thrown into the fire?" he gasped.

"Certainly, O King," one servant answered.

"But I see four men walking around in the fire, men not bound by ropes! And they are all alive! The fourth man looks like a son of the gods." Nebuchadnezzar immediately started to climb the steps. "Come out, Shadrach, Meshach, and Abednego, come out! Now I know that you are servants of the Most High God."

When the three men heard the king's voice, they came out of the fire, only to be met by a crowd that couldn't believe their eyes. There were Shadrach, Meshach, and

Abednego, alive and well! Not a hair on their heads had been singed by the fire, their robes were not burned, and not one man smelled like he had been near a roaring fire.

Nebuchadnezzar then rushed to their sides, grabbing their hands in his.

"Praise be to the God of Shadrach, Meshach, and Abednego!" the king cried. "He has sent His angel to be with you in the furnace and rescue you. What kind of God do you serve? You who were ready to die rather than bow down before any other statue!"

Turning around to face the people, the king cleared his throat. "Today I make a new command to my people. If anyone says anything against the God of Shadrach, Meshach, and Abednego, that person will surely die. No other god can save like their God!"

At that, Aliabad and his fellow astrologers made a quick exit from the scene and were not seen for many days. But Shadrach, Meshach, and Abednego—Hananiah, Mishael, and Azariah—were still in a daze. They had been saved again by their God, saved again for a reason.

That day, the king promoted Hananiah, Mishael, and Azariah, giving them even more important titles than before. And that night, the three men prayed for Nebuchadnezzar that he, too, would worship the God that saves—before it was too late.*

---

* King Nebuchadnezzar had no idea how right he was when he
  said the fourth man in the furnace was "a son of the gods"

or, as some Bibles state, "a Son of God." Many Bible scholars say that Jesus Christ, the Son of God, who would not be born on earth for more than six hundred years, was in the furnace with Shadrach, Meshach, and Abednego. The reason is found in Isaiah 43:2 (NKJV): "I will be with you. . . when you walk through the fire, you shall not be burned, nor shall the flame scorch you." The Old Testament foretold many things about Jesus, all of which Jesus has done or will do.

CHAPTER 4

Thunderheads hung just above the palace of Nebuchadnezzar waiting to burst open with welcome rain. But the stormy weather had little to do with the king's lack of sleep.

"I haven't seen the king so upset about a dream since—" one servant whispered to another, only to be interrupted by Aliabad, who now entered the chambers.

"Yes, don't remind me about that dream, at least not at this hour! And anyway, that was years ago," the astrologer added.

"Aliabad, is that you? Come here, please come here," came the strangely quiet voice of the king. The king was sitting hunched over on his throne, his head in his hands. "I need you to call all of the magicians here—at once."

Aliabad did not have time to hide the surprise from his face. Bowing quickly, he turned and left the chambers and returned a short time later with every magician he could find. Everyone except Daniel. "Tell us your dream, O King, and we will provide our usual excellent interpretation," Aliabad stated grandly, bowing again to the floor.

But a short time later, the astrologers left the king's chambers, their shoulders slumped and their feet dragging, now reduced to whispering insults to each other.

"That kind of dream is your specialty, Habib, not mine!"

"You have no specialty, Sarik, except eating perhaps!"

"Eating? You could give a pig nightmares!"

Aliabad cut short the two bickering astrologers and motioned the group to look down below. Running across the courtyard was Daniel, his robes flying, being taken by Arioch to the chambers of Nebuchadnezzar.

"Why is the king calling *him* now?" Aliabad whispered bitterly.

"As if you don't know," Sarik said under his breath.

"But as the *chief* astrologer—" Aliabad rolled his eyes as if to belittle Daniel's promotion over him—"why wasn't Belteshazzar called first? This time I feel our 'friend' Belteshazzar will not have a ready answer for the king." A sly smile spread over Aliabad's face.

"Maybe the king doesn't really want to know what this dream was about," Habib suggested wisely. "I mean, that would explain why he called us first."

Shrugging their shoulders, the astrologers returned to their rooms, secretly hoping their "services" wouldn't be required anytime soon.

Daniel found the king in much the same way as the astrologers had minutes earlier. *This dream is worse, much worse than the last,* Daniel thought to himself. *God in heaven, please give me wisdom and courage!*

"Belteshazzar, chief of the magicians, I know that the spirit of the holy gods is in you. I know that no mystery is too great for you," Nebuchadnezzar began.

Immediately Daniel was troubled. Even though everyone

in the palace knew that he had been promoted to chief of the magicians, the spirit of one God, not many, controlled his life. Obviously, the king had not learned much in his past encounters with the God of Daniel, Hananiah, Mishael, and Azariah.

Maybe, thought Daniel, *this time God will change the stubborn king's heart.*

The king looked terrified as his eyes roamed the room. He then motioned Daniel to come closer, as if anyone else overhearing this dream might spell disaster. "Here is my dream, then. Interpret it for me.

"I was lying on my bed and there before me stood a tree, an enormous, strong tree, the top branches of which seemed to touch the sky.

"The leaves of the tree were beautiful, and there was more fruit hanging from the branches than you could imagine. Under the tree, animals found shelter, and birds rested on the mighty branches."

The king paused to catch his breath and then continued. "Then I saw an angel coming down from heaven! And this angel ordered the tree cut down, all the leaves stripped off, and the fruit scattered everywhere. Then the animals ran away, and the birds flew off to find another tree."

"Was there nothing left of the tree?" Daniel asked.

"I was just getting to that. The angel then ordered that the stump and the roots of the tree be left in the field and bound with iron and bronze. As if speaking to a person, the angel said to the stump that it would live with the animals and that its mind would be changed from that of a man to the mind of an animal for seven years."

"Is that the dream?" Daniel asked.

"Not quite. By then there were many angels in the sky, and all they could say was that God is ruler over the kingdoms of men. God gives to anyone He wishes, and He also sets over His people the lowliest of men. That is the dream, Belteshazzar, the dream none of my astrologers could interpret."

Daniel's face had lost its color. Feeling he was about to faint, he sat down—and then said nothing for almost an hour. King Nebuchadnezzar could wait no longer.

"Belteshazzar, do not let my dream or its meaning upset you so much."

"My king, if only the dream were meant for your enemies and not for you!" Daniel cried. "But the tree you saw, the beautiful, healthy tree whose branches reached the sky, that tree is you, O King. You have become great and strong, and your empire reaches to distant parts of the earth."

"And what is so terrible about that, Belteshazzar?"

"But you are also the stump and the roots of the tree. You will be driven from your kingdom and will live with the wild animals. You will eat grass like cattle and be drenched by the rains from heaven."

"But my kingdom is so powerful! How could anyone take this away from me, the great Nebuchadnezzar?" Seizing a bunch of grapes, he plopped several into his mouth at once.

"There is more, my king. Seven years will pass before you—the once mighty king—bow before God. Seven years will pass before you finally believe that God is the ruler over all the kingdoms of men and gives them to whomever He wishes. The roots of the tree were not destroyed for a reason. Your kingdom will be restored to you when you finally believe that only God rules your empire."

"When will this all take place? I can see no armies about to attack, only a thunderstorm."

"I cannot tell. I only know this: Ask God to forgive you for your wicked deeds. Be kind to those who are poor and sick. Maybe then this dream will not come true."

As Daniel left the king's chambers, he glanced over his shoulder for a last look at the sleepless Nebuchadnezzar. A larger tray of many varieties of grapes had been placed by his feet, but the king was unaware of it. Servants hovered on either side of him, but the king seemed to ignore them. Fans of peacock feathers held by maidservants swayed up and down to no reaction from the dazed Nebuchadnezzar.

And then a bolt of lightning seemed to slice the room in half, followed seconds later by a crashing boom of thunder— and the cries of a king pleading with his gods.

With every passing month, Daniel watched for changes in King Nebuchadnezzar. But now twelve months had passed— one whole year—and the king was still thinking clearly, still very much in charge of his empire, and, if possible, even more powerful than ever.

Many wars had been fought, and many years had gone by since Daniel had been taken captive and brought to Babylon. And now Babylon was at peace. Life was good for the king, and he knew it.

Nebuchadnezzar had forgotten Daniel's advice, and he had forgotten the words of the angels in his dream: "God gives the kingdoms of men to anyone He wishes and sets over them the lowliest of men."

On this cloudless day, one year after his dream, King Nebuchadnezzar was on the roof of his palace, enjoying the magnificent view of Babylon. And it was a view like no other! The city formed a perfect square, fifteen miles in length on every side, with wide streets and towering buildings. The surging Euphrates River ran right through the middle of the city and under the city walls to the plain, the result of Babylonian engineering.

Positioned between two of the more than two hundred fifty watchtowers on the roof, the king felt safe as well as powerful. And seated beside a now graying Daniel, his most trusted adviser, he felt nothing could go wrong with this day. And then a thought came to him, a thought that had to be spoken.

Standing, with his arms outstretched, Nebuchadnezzar proclaimed, "Is not this the great Babylon, built by my mighty power and for the glory of my majesty?"

Nebuchadnezzar's words seemed to hang in the still air.

Then a voice was heard, a voice that didn't come from the roof or the city streets below. A voice that came from heaven.

"This is what is decreed for you, King Nebuchadnezzar: Your royal authority has been taken from you. You will be driven away from people and will live with the wild animals.

"You will eat grass like cattle. Seven years will pass before you say that God rules over the kingdoms of men and gives them to anyone He wishes."

Turning to look at the king's reaction, Daniel couldn't believe his eyes. For immediately, the once mighty Nebuchadnezzar had become exactly as the creature described in the dream.

"Help, someone, help!" Daniel yelled to the guards, who nearly dropped their spears when they saw the king.

There on the floor of the roof, still in his robes, was King Nebuchadnezzar, sniffing the ground for food and making growling sounds. Daniel and the guards moved away from him, trying again and again to speak to him, but it was no use. Nebuchadnezzar simply bared his teeth and lashed out at them with his jeweled hand, now more like a paw.

It took several guards to finally move the king down to his rooms. But like the wild animal that he had become, it was impossible to keep the king in one place. When, after many days, the king's wife, sons, daughters, and servants realized they could not control him, the king was set free in the wilderness outside the city gates of Babylon.

Only the birds and beasts that roamed the desert could

observe the changes in the once feared king. His lavish robes had long been torn away, and his skin had become as thick as leather. The once glorious mane of hair that had been fit to cushion the crown of an empire now resembled the feathers of an eagle. And his fingernails and toenails—once filed and oiled by adoring servants—looked like the overgrown claws of a bird.

Day after day, week after week, and year after year, Nebuchadnezzar lived the life of an animal. He ate what grass he could find, much like a cow, and his body was washed by the dew from heaven. Living like he had lost his mind, not to mention his beloved kingdom of Babylon, the once proud king kept his head down, looking only for his next meal.

And seven years passed.

The day after seven years had gone by, Nebuchadnezzar raised his eyes to heaven, and immediately God changed his mind back to that of a man. He stood up and stretched out his arms. And then he fell back on the ground.

"O Most High God, I praise and honor You, You who live forever! Your kingdom is eternal, lasting from generation to generation. All the peoples of the earth are nothing compared to You. And yes, now I know that You do as You please with the powers of heaven and the peoples of the earth."

And then, wrapping an animal skin about his body, King Nebuchadnezzar started walking back to the city of Babylon. Remembering the stump in his dream, whose roots had not been destroyed, he knew he would sit again on his throne, but not as the same man as before.

That same day, Daniel was again on the palace roof, staring out at the city but not looking at anything in particular. On the other side of the roof, he heard some commotion, the sound of feet running toward him. Turning, he saw one of Nebuchadnezzar's oldest and most trusted servants, holding his sides, obviously out of breath.

"Master Belteshazzar, come quickly! He is back, he is back!"

"Who are you talking about?"

And then Daniel knew. Seven years had passed. He ran down the stairs faster than he had in years, rounding the corners in a flurry, making his way to the king's chambers.

Standing there, in the middle of the room was Nebuchadnezzar. He had on one of his former robes, which was now several sizes too big. His face was deeply tanned, but his eyes sparkled. And as he grabbed Daniel's hand, Daniel felt the coarse, rough skin.

"O King, you are here, just as in your dream!" Daniel said excitedly.

"Yes, Belteshazzar, I have been restored, just as your God—and mine—promised." Daniel was about to say something, but the king stopped him. "Please, let me finish. My pride in myself prevented me from knowing God; I now know that. And only God is able to humble those who think they are more powerful than He. Now I just want to spend the rest of my days praising God and thanking Him for allowing me to serve Him."

And so it was that Nebuchadnezzar continued to reign as king of Babylon until his death. Nobles from near and far sought an audience with him, and his reputation and wealth grew with each passing year. But always, he gave praise to God—the God who, after three powerful encounters, had changed his life.

CHAPTER 5

The palace of Babylon had become a lonely place for Daniel. Many years had passed since Nebuchadnezzar ruled the empire, and many years had passed since a godly king sat on the throne. Now in the year 539 B.C., few in the palace remembered the courage and faith of Daniel and his three friends, Hananiah, Mishael, and Azariah. Or even knew who they were.

Daniel and his friends were simply old men, all around eighty years old, who somehow, sometime, had earned the respect of a long-ago ruler.

Would they ever be allowed to return home to Jerusalem? Or had God planned for them to live out their days here? Until recently, they had no reason to hope. But now there was talk throughout the palace that the armies of the Medes and Persians were nearing the famous city walls of Babylon.

Seated together in one of the palace's many gardens, the four friends were troubled. *Has anyone told the new king about Nebuchadnezzar's first dream?* they wondered. *The one of the statue?* Nebuchadnezzar was the head of gold, but after him came the kingdom of Medo-Persia, the Medes and the Persians.

The great kingdoms of Media and Persia lay almost directly to the east of the kingdom of Babylon. In 550 B.C.,

255

Cyrus the Great of Persia had conquered Media, and now, together with General Darius the Mede, he turned his attention to Babylon. Since the death of Nebuchadnezzar, Cyrus knew Babylon was not the force it once was. And if he conquered Babylon, the world could be his very soon.

"Do you think one of us should warn King Belshazzar? Or even King Nabonidus when he returns? Maybe if Belshazzar prayed to God, this war might be delayed," suggested Hananiah.

"God has not directed me to do that," Daniel answered slowly. "And we all know that God is not welcome in the king's chambers—at least, not yet."

"You are right as always, my friend," Azariah said. "And what is welcome in the king's chambers. . ." With sadness in their eyes, they all shook their heads.

Two kings, father and son, now shared the throne of Babylon. The father, King Nabonidus, who was married to the daughter of Nebuchadnezzar, ruled the empire outside the city of Babylon. Belshazzar, his son, ruled the city from the throne in the palace.

Even though King Belshazzar was the grandson of Nebuchadnezzar, he had little in common with the former king. Instead of keeping Babylon secure from its enemies, he spent his time entertaining at lavish parties, drinking too much wine, and worshipping his many idols—idols of silver, gold, wood, and stone.

Although he was aware that Babylon would soon be at

war, Belshazzar made a typical entrance, skipping into his chambers while humming a silly tune, only to meet a sea of dark and serious faces. The faces of his military advisers.

"Why so sad today? Haven't you heard—but surely you were invited—tonight I'm giving my biggest party yet!" Belshazzar could not keep from giggling. He had obviously been drinking, and it was early in the day.

"King Belshazzar, the news of the Medes and Persians is not good. In fact, spies report that our enemies may attack Babylon tonight," one adviser stated.

"If only I were on a first-name basis with what's-his-name. Or who's the other one?" Lost in thought, the king began twirling a lock of his short, curly hair.

"Cyrus, you mean? The king of Persia?" One adviser stared amazed at the king.

"And Darius, the general of the Medes?" another added.

"Yes, him and him. I mean, they're welcome to join us, but perhaps that would be a bit much!" And at that, Belshazzar dissolved into fits of laughter.

"King Belshazzar," another adviser began, "perhaps tonight is not the best night for your, er, celebration. Our spies report the Medes and Persians have the best weapons and more soldiers than—"

"STOP! How dare you ruin my party! Now go, all of you. I need to speak to the chefs and wine stewards about more important matters."

That night in the great banquet hall of the palace, the

tables were set for a thousand guests. Silver plates and gold trays gleamed in the candlelight, not to be outdone by the sparkling jewels worn by all present. Only the wealthiest of Babylon were there, and each one wanted to be noticed.

As King Belshazzar sipped from his oversized wine goblet, he was pleased with the way the party was going. But then a thought crossed his mind, a thought that would not go away. These guests were used to being served on the finest silver and gold. Tonight, the night of his grandest party, he would not disappoint them.

After whispering an urgent order to the servant by his side, the king sat back in his chair. Why hadn't he thought of this before?

Later, as the servants of the king paraded into the hall, each carrying a tray, gasps could be heard from the guests. For on every tray, polished to a rare sheen, were the most magnificent gold goblets they had ever seen.

"King Belshazzar, where have you been keeping these? They are exquisite!" exclaimed one noble seated at the king's table.

"And what are these writings on the goblets? From what distant land did these come?" another guest inquired.

The king was beside himself with pride. What a brilliant move this had been to bring in the goblets stolen from the holy temple in Jerusalem—goblets brought to Babylon seventy years ago and never used until now.

Standing, Belshazzar watched until each guest had his

own goblet, and each goblet was filled with wine. "Drink up!" he cried out, almost laughing. "And as we drink, let us make a toast to the gods of Babylon, the gods who have given us so much!"

As all the guests sipped the wine from the rare golden goblets, out of nowhere the fingers of a human hand appeared. No arm, no body, no legs, no head—just the fingers of a human hand, floating in the air.

Dancing amid the shadows cast by the candlelight, the mysterious hand traveled between the tables of the banquet hall. When the hand neared the walls, the shadows the fingers themselves created were the scariest of all. The hand seemed far larger than any human hand, and far more dangerous.

The room fell silent, except for the nervous rattling of goblets and silver on the tables and the gasps that escaped the open mouths of the bejeweled guests. One servant dropped his tray and scurried from the hall. Several women fainted and dropped to the floor from their seats, sending other servants hurrying to their aid.

Even so, all eyes were fastened on the mysterious hand and fingers, and what they would do next.

Then, on the plaster wall behind the king, the fingers began to write a message—a message that consisted of four words. And then the hand disappeared.

Belshazzar sat frozen, his face the color of ashes. But under the table, his knees began knocking together.

When he finally raised himself to stand, his legs would

not support him, and he nearly collapsed to the floor, grabbing the table for balance. "Send in my astrologers immediately!" the king ordered, after clearing his throat several times. "Whoever can tell me what these words mean will be clothed in purple and have a gold chain placed around his neck. Furthermore, that person will be made the third highest ruler in the kingdom!"

But when the astrologers examined all four words of the message in great detail, they could not begin to tell the king what the words meant.

At that moment, King Belshazzar's mother, Queen Nitocris, the daughter of Nebuchadnezzar, entered the banquet hall. Looking every inch like the mother of a king, with her graying hair piled high on her head and her gown of lavender silk, Nitocris walked slowly toward her son, her back straight. While she nodded her greetings to a select few of the nobles she passed, she clearly had not come to join the party.

"My son, the king, I pray to the gods that you will live forever! You look so pale, but there is no reason to be afraid," she said to Belshazzar. "There is a man in your kingdom—in the palace—who has the spirit of the holy gods in him.

"In the time of your grandfather, this man was found to be as wise as the gods. In fact, Nebuchadnezzar appointed him chief of all the astrologers."

"His name, Mother? Do you remember his name?" The king was impatient as always.

"Ah, yes, I do indeed. My father called him Belteshazzar,

but his Hebrew name was Daniel. He could interpret dreams, explain riddles, and solve the most difficult problems. You must call for Daniel."

Snapping his fingers, the king ordered that Daniel, whoever he was, be found immediately and brought to the banquet hall. *This Daniel is probably some ancient creature who once had a gift,* Belshazzar thought to himself. Of course, he had to send for him—or lose the respect of all the nobles at the party. His own mother had recommended Daniel, after all.

And then Daniel was led inside the hall. Still a tall man with perfect posture, his white hair flowed in the air as he walked briskly toward the king and bowed before him. The king looked into the piercing blue eyes of Daniel, and then looked away. His grandfather had not been wrong about this man.

Upon entering the banquet hall, Daniel could not help noticing the abundance of silver and gold around him. The silver plates and serving utensils, the golden trays heaped high with rich foods—the same dishes he and his friends had rejected!—and the bracelets, earrings, rings, and necklaces adorning all the nobles and their wives.

And then his eyes traveled to the golden goblets filled with wine, the rare goblets never before seen in Babylon. Daniel's eyes filled with tears—and then his fists became clenched with anger.

These goblets had been stolen by Nebuchadnezzar from

God's temple in Jerusalem. These goblets were only to be used by the high priests to worship God. These goblets were holy!

To make matters far worse, these goblets were being used to drink from—and to toast the false gods of Belshazzar and the Babylonians. *God can wait no longer,* Daniel thought to himself. *God has to show His power!*

Now face-to-face with Belshazzar, Daniel looked straight into his eyes. The eyes of a coward. The eyes of a man who thinks only of himself and his riches and his pleasures.

"Are you Daniel, one of the captives my grandfather the king brought to Babylon from Israel?" Belshazzar began.

"I am he, O King," Daniel answered.

"I have heard that the spirit of the gods is in you and that you are very wise. Perhaps you can still be of use to me, the grandson of Nebuchadnezzar. . . ."

Daniel said nothing. Clenching and unclenching his fists, he simply stared into the darting eyes of this desperate ruler.

"Out of nowhere, fingers appeared and began writing on this wall, and then they disappeared," the king continued, motioning to the wall behind him. "My astrologers, who possess the finest minds for thousands of miles, have already examined this extraordinary message, and none of them can tell me what it means."

Daniel turned his attention to the wall behind the king. There was other writing on the wall, as well, words praising King Belshazzar, as was the custom of the day. But the four words written by the hand of God were still clearly visible to him:

Mene, Mene, Tekel, Parsin

"If you can tell me what these words mean," the king went on, repeating himself, "you will be clothed in purple, and a gold chain will be placed around your neck. Furthermore, you will be made the third highest ruler in the kingdom."

A pained look crossed Daniel's face. "You may keep your gifts for yourself—or give them to someone else. I will tell you what the writing means without a reward."

Gasps and whispers could be heard throughout the hall, and then silence. Sitting on the edge of their seats, the guests waited breathlessly for the strange, white-haired wise man to speak. Belshazzar eased himself into his padded chair.

"The Most High God, the God of heaven, gave your grandfather Nebuchadnezzar great power and splendor. Because of all that God gave him, your grandfather was a mighty and feared ruler. Those he wanted to put to death, he put to death; those he wanted to save, he saved. But when he started to think too much of himself, when he became filled with pride, God took away his glory. Do you remember what happened to your grandfather, O King?"

Daniel's history lesson was beginning to have an effect on King Belshazzar. The king knew that his grandfather had lost his mind. Was that going to happen to him, too?

"Yes, I have heard the stories," the king answered quietly. Then he laughed nervously. "Who hasn't?"

"Stories are sometimes made up and sometimes true. But what happened to your grandfather, the mighty and feared Nebuchadnezzar, was God's plan! Your grandfather was driven away from people and given the mind of an animal. He lived with the wild donkeys and ate grass like cattle. And his body was washed with the dew from heaven—until he worshipped the Most High God! Only God rules over the kingdoms of men and sets over these kingdoms anyone He wishes," Daniel said, pausing to catch his breath.

"You may have heard the stories, King Belshazzar, but you have not learned anything from them. Instead, you have set yourself up against the God of heaven!"

The banquet hall suddenly was transformed into a beehive as anxious voices competed with each other, echoing off the walls of the room. *These nobles are only pretending to like King Belshazzar,* thought Daniel as he gazed from table to table. *As soon as they think he's going to be deposed from power, how quickly they are ready to follow someone else.* But Daniel was not finished with the sad and scared looking king. Not yet.

Looking only at the king, Daniel continued. "You had the goblets from God's holy temple in Jerusalem brought to you tonight, to you and your nobles, so you could drink your wine and toast your gods—gods made from gold, bronze, iron, wood, and stone—gods that cannot see or hear or understand!" Daniel almost spit the words from his mouth.

The king seemed to sink even lower in his chair.

"But you did not honor the God Who holds your life in His hands. And for that reason, God sent the fingers that wrote on your wall."

All eyes were now on the message, the four words that no one could interpret:

Mene, Mene, Tekel, Parsin

"The message, as you know, is easy to read: 'Mene, mene, tekel, parsin,' or numbered, numbered, weighed, and divided. 'Mene, mene' means that God has numbered the days of your kingdom, and He has brought it to an end. 'Tekel' says that you have been weighed on the scales by God and found to be evil. And finally, 'parsin'—your kingdom will be divided and given to the Medes and Persians."

Oddly enough, at that moment the king stood and placed on Daniel's shoulders the purple robe. Around Daniel's wrinkled neck, Belshazzar placed a heavy gold chain. And then in front of the thousand nobles, he promoted Daniel to third in his kingdom.

Daniel had made his wishes known to King Belshazzar. He did not want to be rewarded for what he did not—and could not—do. Only God could interpret dreams; only God could send fingers to write on a wall; only God could tell a king when his reign was over.

Even though he accepted the king's luxurious gifts, Daniel did not stay at the party. And even though Daniel had warned Belshazzar that the end of his kingdom was here, the party continued. Wine flowed from giant casks and into the golden goblets as the king and his guests strayed even further from the will of God.

Outside the palace, however, the clear thinking of the Medes and Persians was about to pay off. A plan had been hatched days earlier to change the course of the Euphrates River, the river that flowed *under* the city walls of Babylon. By stopping the flow of the river, the riverbed under the wall would eventually dry up.

Tonight, the night of Belshazzar's celebration, the riverbed was pronounced completely dry—and that meant everything. The armies of the Medes and the Persians could enter Babylon under the famous wall instead of trying to overtake it, a feat that would have been almost impossible.

As loud laughter rang from the palace porticoes in the early morning hours, the troops led by Darius the Mede and Cyrus of Persia completely surrounded the palace. The city was theirs—except for the king and his family.

Their swords waving in the air, the soldiers ran into the banquet hall, sending the drunken nobles sprawling on the floor. Those who could still stand weakly tried to run away, but they did not get very far. Goblets crashed to the floor, and food went flying as the soldiers made their way to the king.

But King Belshazzar put up little fight. He was captured easily and taken away to be killed. Later, King Nabonidus would also surrender to Cyrus the Great.

Belshazzar's days had indeed been numbered, his deeds had been weighed, and now his kingdom of Babylon was no more. The golden head of the image in Nebuchadnezzar's first dream had been toppled, as another of Daniel's prophecies came true.

As Daniel prayed in the early morning hours, again facing Jerusalem, he wondered if his years in Babylon were over. *Dear God, will I be sent home at last?* he prayed. *Or can You still use an old man like me?*

CHAPTER 6

The answer to Daniel's prayer came much sooner than he expected. Word of Daniel's powers—"the power of the Most High God," Daniel always corrected—had spread quickly around the Medo-Persian empire, and that included the new king who sat in the palace of Babylon.

Soon after General Darius the Mede had been appointed king of Babylon by Cyrus the Great, he called Daniel to his chambers. Darius had come up with a new plan to rule his portion of the empire, and he wanted Daniel, with all his wisdom, to play a significant role. "I want you to know, Daniel, that I will not take no for an answer. Yes, you are older than my other advisers, but you have proven yourself, more than anyone else, capable of a high position in this kingdom."

Daniel couldn't believe his ears after all those years when no one knew him!

"I am honored to serve you, King Darius," Daniel replied.

"Then listen, for here is my plan: The kingdom of Babylon will be divided into one hundred twenty provinces to be governed by one hundred twenty satraps (that is to say, princes). These one hundred twenty satraps will report to three presidents, and those presidents will report back to me, as king. Daniel, I would like you to serve as one of the three presidents."

Daniel was aware that the king was studying his face for his reaction. *Surely this must be God's plan,* Daniel thought to himself. *Only God could put me in this position!*

"Again, I would be honored to serve you in whatever way you desire," he answered.

"Good, that's settled then. You will receive further instructions in the days to come. I know you will serve me well, Daniel, just as you served Nebuchadnezzar and Belshazzar during their reigns."

In the months that followed, Daniel did not disappoint King Darius. Time and again, the satraps who reported to Daniel returned to their provinces amazed at his decisions and his wisdom. He settled all disputes fairly and never held grudges against anyone. If the satraps failed to collect the necessary taxes, for example, Daniel always gave them a second chance, and even a third, to prove themselves.

Daniel's performance as a president of Babylon was about to be rewarded. As he entered the king's chambers, Daniel faced a beaming King Darius, whose smile stretched from ear to ear. Daniel could not help noticing that standing around the throne were the other two presidents as well as several satraps. But their smiles were only polite—and forced.

"Daniel, Daniel, the honor of your presence is desired!" the king began warmly.

Daniel bowed slowly before the throne.

"You have performed your duties as president to the best of your abilities, which is to say, you have a most excellent spirit. Most excellent! And so today I am pleased to tell you of my future plans for you. Daniel, I am arranging to put the entire kingdom under your control. No longer will you serve simply as a president. You will rule over all presidents and all satraps!"

Again, Daniel scratched his ear to make sure he had heard correctly. "I am without words, O King. I will be pleased to serve you however you desire."

"Then say no more!" the king cried, clapping his hands. "I'll start to make the necessary arrangements. The rest of you may go now, except Daniel. I need to ask your opinion on some pressing matters."

Shooting a glance at the presidents and satraps as they left the chambers, Daniel felt strangely troubled.

Their heads bent and their hands behind their backs, the presidents and satraps moved slowly down the broad pillar-lined hallway of the palace. "We cannot talk here," whispered Tobruk, one of the presidents, as he eyed one of Darius's guards.

"Meet at my home at sunset," Abbad the satrap suggested. "We have much to discuss!"

That evening, the candles in Abbad's home burned low as the men weighed many plans. Plain and simple, they were jealous of Daniel. They wanted what he had, especially the power and position that come when one is highly thought of by the king. And if they could not achieve that—and it was obvious that right now they could not—they would find a way to bring Daniel down.

"Abbad, you check how he keeps track of the money of his provinces. Any mistakes and we would have an instant case," Tobruk advised.

"Yes, money is the place to start. Besides, as far as we know, Daniel has never married, he has never been found to be drunk or foolish, and he has never lied to anyone. All he does is read, study, and pray to his God, the Most High God he calls Him," Abbad said.

Tobruk scratched his chin, deep in thought. "Maybe that is the key to our Daniel," he said with an evil glint in his eye.

Days later, the group of presidents and satraps met again in the home of Abbad.

"Upon checking all the records Daniel has kept, I have yet to find a single mistake. Every single shekel can be accounted for, my friends. Daniel is a man the king could trust."

"I was afraid of that," Tobruk stated. "So we go to plan B. We will create a new law—a law that goes against the law of the God of Daniel!"

Again the candles burned low that night in the home of Abbad as the small group of presidents and satraps quickly wrote the new law. Too much time had passed already, they decided. They must see the king early in the morning, perhaps before he was fully awake!

With Tobruk leading the way, the group entered the king's chambers the next day, bowing as low as they could before a sleepy-eyed King Darius. "O King, live forever!"

Tobruk began, sounding the usual greeting. "The royal presidents and satraps have all agreed that you should sign a new law that all peoples should obey, starting immediately." Tobruk hoped the lie of this statement was not too obvious.

"Law? This early in the morning? But what is so pressing that I must make such a decision now? Surely this can wait, perhaps until Daniel sees it." The king tried to focus on the group before him.

The presidents and satraps looked at one another with alarm. Abbad then stepped closer to the throne. "King Darius, this new law will strengthen the power of the new empire in Babylon. You have come to this kingdom a stranger. But with this law all peoples will feel bound closer to you. They will worship you; they will adore you!"

Darius settled himself contentedly in his chair. *Perhaps what Abbad said is true.* "What exactly is this law?"

"Simply this, O King: Anyone who prays to any god or man except to you during the next thirty days will be thrown into the lions' den," said Tobruk, bowing again. "King Darius, issue the decree and put it in writing so that it cannot be changed, according to the laws of the Medes and Persians." He then handed the papyrus to the king.

Without further discussion, King Darius placed his official seal on the law.

Tobruk had made a special point of mentioning the laws of the Medes and Persians for a reason. Unlike the laws of the Babylonians, the laws of the Medes and Persians could not be reversed, even by the king himself. *Daniel will not control this kingdom,* Tobruk thought to himself, smiling slyly. *No one can escape ferocious lions, especially hungry ones.*

The lions of Mesopotamia, the region that included Babylon, were prized and feared. Kings were known to hunt them for sport, but lions were also used to kill criminals. In Persia, and now Babylon, lions were even kept and fed in special parks, to be used whenever the situation arose.

Now the situation had arisen, according to this scheming group of presidents and satraps, and all they had to do was catch Daniel in the act of praying.

Daniel was reading in his room in the palace when he was interrupted by several soft knocks on the door. Slipping into his sandals, he made his way slowly to answer. He knew who it was, after all, or he had it narrowed down to three possibilities.

"Mishael, come in, come in. Shall I have some tea prepared for us?"

"No, I cannot stay long today. I have heard some news that is, well. . ."

"Please, tell me. Look what we have been through all these years!"

"You are right, of course. A servant just brought me word that King Darius has signed a most unusual law, a law written by all the presidents and satraps, but clearly not by you."

"What kind of law?" Daniel had suddenly become curious, and his cloudy blue eyes crinkled at the corners.

Mishael gave him all the details, then hugged him as he left. "Daniel, you do have a choice. Be careful, my friend."

As Daniel sat alone, he considered his "choices," such as they were. He could stop praying for thirty days, or he could hide while praying, making sure no one saw him. Or he could continue as he always had, praying three times a day, gazing through his window open to the west, to Jerusalem.

The choice was not hard for Daniel.

And so he continued praying, just as he had for almost eighty years, unaware of who might be watching him. A few days later, the presidents and satraps had all the evidence they needed against Daniel. They had seen him praying to his God, and they had listened to his prayer:

"O God, You Who are Most High in heaven, please help me to be strong, and to never stop worshipping You. For You alone are my God."

King Darius was deep in thought when the same group of presidents and satraps approached him. The king opened his eyes and looked straight into their overeager faces. "Well, what is it? What is so important that you disturb my thinking?"

"Did you not issue a decree just days ago, O King, a law that all must worship only you for the next thirty days or risk being thrown into the lions' den?" Abbad asked bravely, all the while knowing the answer.

"Of course! And you were all there, as I recall. The law still stands, a law that even I cannot change." About to lose his patience, the king swatted violently at a bug on the arm of his chair.

"I am sorry to report, O King, that Daniel—he that is to oversee this kingdom—pays no attention to you or to the law you put in writing," Tobruk continued, then paused to make sure the king was listening. "Daniel still prays three times a day to his God!"

The king stared at the men before him, but his eyes were not focused on any of them. His mouth opened slightly, and beads of perspiration began to appear on his forehead. "Be gone, all of you! I need to be alone," Darius declared.

As the men scattered out of the king's chambers, Darius put his head in his hands. *How could I have been so foolish to sign such a law?* he thought desperately. *Daniel is a fine man, a man full of wisdom, a man who does not deserve to die. And now I have sentenced him to the lions' den!*

Raising his hands to the tiled ceiling, Darius yelled out loud, "I must do something! There must be some way I can save Daniel—and I only have until sundown." Pacing back and forth, he suddenly stopped in his tracks. "Quick, send in my legal advisers!" he ordered a servant.

But as sundown approached, the king was no closer to finding a way out of the lions' den for Daniel. A decree such as this, issued according to the laws of the Medes and Persians, had no room for exceptions.

"Bring Daniel to me," the king said sadly, his voice barely above a whisper.

As Daniel was led into the king's chambers, he knew the time had come for his faith to be tested again. Yet unlike King Darius, whose eyes were red and robes twisted around his body, Daniel appeared calm and strong.

"Daniel, today I order you thrown into the lions' den for disobeying the law of the empire. May your God, Whom you serve continually, rescue you!"

And at that the tall, quiet, white-haired gentleman with the wise eyes was led away, closer and closer to the earth-shaking bellows of the hungry beasts.

CHAPTER 7

Terrified by the roars, the king's guards didn't want to get too close to the lions' den themselves. And although Daniel was not holding on to them or showing any fear, still they gave him a mighty push and backed away quickly.

Following the king's orders, a massive stone was then rolled in front of the mouth of the den and placed over the opening. "There's no chance an old guy like that would escape anyway," one guard said to another.

The other guard nodded his agreement.

"If Daniel lasts one minute in there, I'd be surprised!"

Finally, the king arrived and placed his official seal on the stone, applied with wax and his own signet ring, as well as the rings of the presidents and satraps, who were only too happy to be there.

When King Darius returned to his palace later, he hardly looked like the king that he was. Not only were his eyes still red and his robes twisted and falling off his shoulders, but he shuffled his feet and mumbled to himself. Seeing his troubled condition, his personal servants became terribly worried.

"King Darius, the chefs have prepared your favorite dishes for tonight. Simply give the word and the table will be set," one servant began.

"King Darius, the jugglers and dancers from Persia are here, by your special request. Let me call them in to entertain you before dinner," another servant offered.

"King Darius, let me prepare a bath for you. I have laid out on your bed your softest robes," yet another said, a pleading look on his face.

But to all these requests, the king said nothing. And then he stumbled off to his rooms for the night.

At the same time that King Darius was not acting like himself, Daniel was also in a curious situation. He knew he should be afraid—here he was, in the middle of the night, surrounded by heavily muscled beasts, with no hope of human rescue—but he felt strangely at peace. Truly, God had saved his life again.

Earlier that evening, when he had been thrown down into the den, the shock of his fall caused him to pass out briefly. When he awakened, there were several lions sniffing him, their whiskers giving him goose bumps.

Rather than tearing him apart with their bone-crushing jaws, the lions merely seemed to be interested in who he was. Upon realizing that he was completely harmless—and without many teeth!—they left him alone, retreating to an opposite corner of the den.

Amazed at the lions, Daniel looked up only to discover that he was not alone. A few yards away stood a shining being clothed in white, an angel sent from God. As if to answer the question in Daniel's mind, the angel approached a lion and placed its hands on the animal's mouth and then disappeared from the den.

At that moment Daniel knew, as if he had not fully realized this before. Lying face down in the den, Daniel thanked God over and over again for such a miracle.

All light had left the den by this time, so Daniel curled up in a corner and tried to sleep. But before sleep claimed him, he had one final thought: King Darius is in for the surprise of his life in the morning.

For King Darius, the night was far from restful. After tossing and turning, and pacing around his bed countless times, the king threw on his robes at the first sign of sunrise. Startling his servants who waited outside his rooms, Darius raced to the lions' den. But instead of the usual roars, silence greeted the king.

When he came near the den, Darius cried out hoarsely, "Daniel, Daniel! Has your God, Whom you serve continually, been able to rescue you from the lions?" Tears escaped from his eyes, following the lines down his cheeks and running off his chin.

At that moment, the king heard a voice he thought he'd never hear again—Daniel was alive! "O King, live forever!" Daniel's voice was strong and clear. "My God sent His angel and he shut the mouths of the lions. Do not worry, King Darius. The lions have not hurt me at all. I was found innocent in God's sight, and I have done nothing wrong before you either."

Immediately, King Darius gave the order to have the stone removed and Daniel lifted out of the lions' den. When he saw him, the king raced to his side, placing his hands on Daniel's shoulders.

"Look at you, my trusted friend. There is not a scratch on your body, and even your garments have not been ripped," Darius declared. "You have surely trusted in your God, and your God has delivered you from certain death!"

Then, turning to his guards, Darius gave a most gruesome order. He ordered those presidents and satraps who had plotted against Daniel—Tobruk, Abbad, and the rest—to be thrown themselves into the lions' den. According to the laws of Persia, the families of these men would be thrown into the den, as well.

As Daniel and the king made their way back to the palace, the cries of those sentenced to death could be heard, for the lions were eating them.

Days later, King Darius called for his scribes to come to his chambers. With papyrus in hand, they arrived and began to record a new law for the king. In the words of Darius, this new decree would be sent to "all the peoples, nations, and men of every language throughout the land," that is, the Medo-Persian empire.

"May you prosper greatly!" the king began to dictate. "I issue a decree that in every part of my kingdom, people must fear and worship the God of Daniel. For He is the living God and He endures forever; His kingdom will not be destroyed and will never end. He rescues and He saves; He performs signs and wonders in the heavens and on the earth."

Daniel himself smiled when he read the final sentence. In just a few words, King Darius had learned the power of faith. The king had written, "God has rescued Daniel from the power of the lions."

Such a decree had been a long time coming, especially for Jews like Daniel, Mishael, Hananiah, and Azariah. In so many words, King Darius had now decreed that it was acceptable for Jews to worship their God in any part of the new empire. From this day on, Jews would never be forced to bow down to a golden statue. From this day on, their God would be treated with respect.

Daniel was promptly installed in his new position as chief officer of Babylon, overseeing all one hundred twenty satraps and three presidents. For the next three years, Daniel would serve under Darius and Cyrus the Great, offering his usual wisdom, all in the name of El Elyon, the Most High God.

Daniel would stay in Babylon, but for other Jews, the time had come to return to Judah, and to their homes in Jerusalem.

Dusk was settling on Babylon, that time of day when it seems all buildings and streets are bathed in blue. As Daniel walked slowly down the wide boulevards of the city, he felt the beauty of the moment. But his heart was heavy and sad.

He was taking his time reaching his destination, stopping to greet many people, partly because he did not want this evening to end.

He was on his way, after all, to the home of Hananiah and his family. Mishael and Azariah would be there, too, along with many children, grandchildren, and yes, great-grandchildren.

There would be more food than he could possibly eat, more stories than he could remember to tell, and more reasons to laugh than he had ever found before. And there would be countless pauses when all he would want to do was cry.

In this year of 538 B.C., King Darius had declared that all Jews who wanted to could begin returning to their homeland, to Jerusalem. Daniel, being single and with an esteemed position in the government, felt he could not leave. God's work in Babylon was not finished; he was sure of that.

But his dear friends, after praying all these years facing Jerusalem, could not pass up this opportunity. They were leaving the next day, with their large families in tow, on a journey they had never stopped dreaming about. Their caravans were waiting outside the Ishtar Gate for their departure at first light.

Just before he reached the door to Hananiah's house, Daniel patted the pocket of his robe. *Yes, it is there,* he thought gratefully. *I have not forgotten.*

Hananiah's home was decorated for a festive party, even though all the family belongings had been packed. Candles borrowed from friends and neighbors flickered in their holders on makeshift tables, their flames streaming because of the constant commotion in the rooms. Flowers in vases were in all corners, while above, silk fabric of many colors was hung like streamers across the ceilings, swooping down at points to grace the heads of the taller guests.

As soon as he walked in the door, Daniel became the center of attention. His friends hugged him again and again, and when he looked into their eyes he saw they were filled with tears. How would he ever make it through this evening? How could he say good-bye to the best friends he had ever had?

Later, after several platefuls of delicacies and several rounds of favorite songs, Daniel motioned for his friends to follow him.

With a candle held in one hand, Daniel led Mishael, Hananiah, and Azariah into the garden, directly behind the house. His friends watched with curiosity as Daniel fumbled in his pocket for a minute. "A few words for your journey," he said as he opened his hand to reveal a worn piece of papyrus.

"Shall we guess what it is? You know, Daniel, my eyes

aren't very good," Mishael said.

"Is it a riddle? The answer to a dream I never had?" Azariah was always one for jokes.

Hananiah then spoke up. "No, no, this is something serious. I can tell by the look in Daniel's eyes. He's been planning this for a long time."

Daniel cleared his throat. "You really don't remember? There we were, spending our first day in Nebuchadnezzar's palace, trying to learn that confusing alphabet. . . ."

"Of course!" cried Mishael. "Our names—you wrote what our names meant in Hebrew so that we would never forget. Let me see. . .Mishael, 'who is comparable to God?' There is surely no other god but God. Remember the first time we were almost killed?"

"Only God could interpret the king's dream in time to save us," Azariah added. "Azariah, 'whom God helps.' Only God could give us strength to survive on water and vegetables. God knew that we needed His strength, the strength to follow the faith of our families."

"And my name, Hananiah, 'whom God hath favored.' I think of that meaning, and I am transported back to the fiery furnace. Not a hair on our bodies was burned, my friends, imagine that! And our robes did not even smell of a roaring fire," Hananiah remembered. "Yes, God favored us then, and He has favored us now. We will see Jerusalem again."

"And your name, Daniel?" Mishael then asked.

"Yes, 'God is my judge,' and I answer only to Him. And

that has made a difference here in Babylon, an empire that once worshipped only gods of stone and metal. Because I answer only to Him, God gave me the power to show Nebuchadnezzar—yes, and Belshazzar, too—that there is only one God. And God gave me the strength to continue praying to Him, even though I faced death in the lions' den. When you answer only to God, you can do amazing things. You simply need to have faith."

Daniel paused to catch his breath. Then, tearing the papyrus into three pieces, he handed his friends their "names." "When you reach Jerusalem, no one will know you as Shadrach, Meshach, and Abednego. Godspeed, my friends."

And turning his back on them, Daniel returned to the house to offer his good-byes and then headed out into the night toward home.

If you enjoyed

BIBLE HEROES,

check out these other great
Backpack Books!

GIRLS' CLASSICS
Including *Pocahontas,*
Little Women,
Pollyanna, and *Heidi*

BIBLE HEROINES
Including *Deborah, Ruth,*
Esther, and *Mary*

MODERN HEROES
Including *Corrie ten Boom,*
Eric Liddell, Billy Graham,
and *Luis Palau*

GOD'S AMBASSADORS
Including *Hudson Taylor,*
David Livingstone, Gladys
Aylward, and *Jim Elliot*

CHRISTIAN ADVENTURES
Including *Ben-Hur,*
The Pilgrim's Progress,
Robinson Crusoe, and
The Swiss Family Robinson

AMERICAN HEROES
Including
Roger Williams,
Abraham Lincoln,
Harriet Tubman,
and *Clara Barton*

THE SON OF GOD
Including *Jesus,*
The Miracles of Jesus,
The Parables of Jesus,
and *The Twelve Disciples*

Great reading at a great price–only $3.97 each!

Available wherever books are sold.
Or order from
Barbour Publishing, Inc.
P.O. Box 719
Uhrichsville, Ohio 44683

If ordering by mail,
please add $2.00 to your order for shipping and handling.
Prices are subject to change without notice.